MODE

MINI KNITS

15
Hand Knit Designs
For Children
Aged 3-12

Credits

Photographer: Jesse Wild
Models: Tiegan and Janae
Art Director & Stylist: Georgina Brant

First published in Great Britain in 2020 by
Quail Publishing Limited
Unit 15, Green Farm, Fritwell, Bicester, Oxfordshire, OX27 7QU
E-mail: info@quailstudio.co.uk

Mode Mini Knits
ISBN: 978-1-9162445-8-0

© Rowan 2020
© Quail Publishing Limited

MODE
MINI KNITS

The children in your life will love looking just as stylish as the grown ups in these mini versions of our most popular Mode patterns.

Mix and match our collection of adorable sweaters, cardigans and accessories for a fun and layered look, ideal for a child's trans-seasonal wardrobe.

Featuring irresistibly soft, tactile yarns and a variety of knitting techniques, knitters of all abilities will love creating these stylish and comfortable clothes for little ones.

MODE

Snowdrop | UK 38 DE 74

Dream | UK 42 DE 77

Flo (hat) | UK 44 DE 79
Fifi (scarf) | UK 46 DE 81

Flo (hat) | UK 44 DE 79
Tallulah (scarf) | UK 45 DE 80

Teddy | UK 47 DE 82

Luna | UK 49 DE 84

Silver | UK 53 DE 88

Moon | UK 55 DE 90

Alaska | UK 56 DE 91

Bear | UK 58 DE 94

Ivy | UK 60 DE 96

Haze | UK 64 DE 100

Rosie | UK 66 DE 102

Cub | UK 62 DE 98

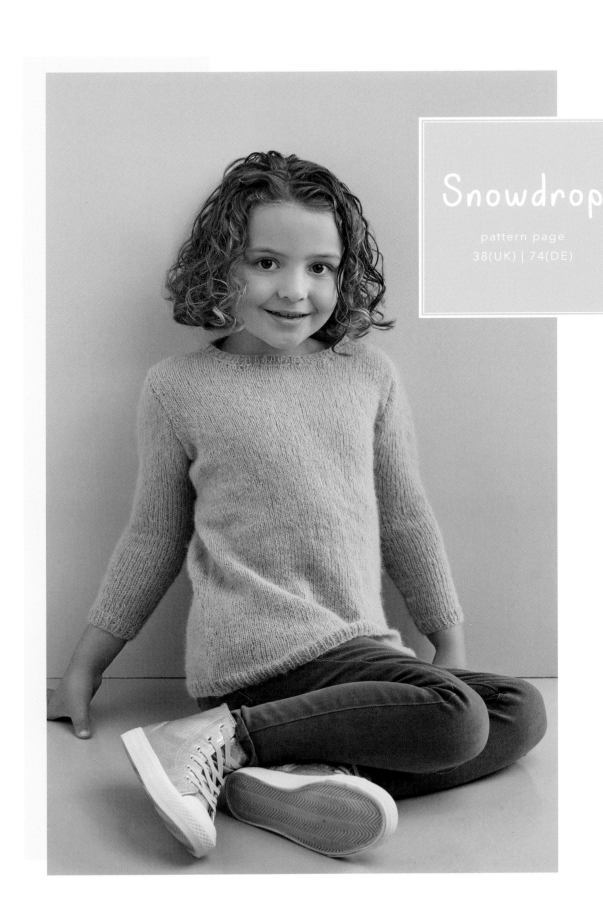

Snowdrop

pattern page
38(UK) | 74(DE)

Dream

pattern page
42(UK) | 77(DE)

Flo
hat ⓐ
pattern page
44(UK) | 79(DE)

Tallulah
scarf ⓑ
pattern page
45(UK) | 80(DE)

Fifi
scarf ⓒ
pattern page
46(UK) | 81(DE)

Teddy

pattern page
47(UK) | 82(DE)

Luna

pattern page
49(UK) | 84(DE)

Silver
cardigan

pattern page
53(UK) | 88(DE)

Tallulah
scarf

pattern page
45(UK) | 80(DE)

Moon

pattern page
55(UK) | 90(DE)

Alaska

pattern page
56(UK) | 91(DE)

Bear

pattern page
58(UK) | 94(DE)

Ivy

pattern page
60(UK) | 96(DE)

Cub

pattern page
62(UK) | 98(DE)

Haze

pattern page
64(UK) | 100(DE)

Rosie
hat ⓐ
pattern page
66(UK) | 102(DE)

Dream
jumper ⓑ
pattern page
42(UK) | 77(DE)

Haze
cardigan ⓒ
pattern page
64(UK) | 100(DE)

Patterns

Snowdrop
quail studio
★ ☆ ☆ ☆

SIZE

To fit age	3-4	5-6	7-8	9-10	11-12	years
To fit chest						
	53-56	59-61	64-66	69-74	76-79	cm
	21-22	23-24	25-26	27-29	30-31	in
Actual chest measurement of garment						
	69	74	79	86	93	cm
	27	29	31	34	36½	in

YARN
Rowan Alpaca Classic

Round neck tunic						
	5	5	6	7	8	x 25gm

(photographed in Soft Satin 116)

V neck tunic						
	5	5	6	7	8	x 25gm

(photographed in Snowflake White 115)

NEEDLES
1 pair 3¼mm (no 10) (US 3) needles
1 pair 3¾mm (no 9) (US 5) needles
3¼mm (no 10) (US 3) circular needle no more than 30 cm long
(or set of 4 double-pointed needles)

EXTRAS
Stitch holders
Stitch markers

TENSION
23 sts and 31 rows to 10 cm / 4 in measured over st st using 3¾mm (US 5) needles.

Round neck tunic
BACK
Using 3¼mm (US 3) needles cast on 79 [85: 91: 99: 107] sts.
Row 1 (RS): K1, *P1, K1, rep from * to end.
Row 2: P1, *K1, P1, rep from * to end.
These 2 rows form rib.
Cont in rib for a further 6 [6: 8: 8: 8] rows, ending with RS facing for next row.
Change to 3¾mm (US 5) needles.
Beg with a K row, now work in st st throughout as folls:
Cont straight until back meas 35 [39: 43: 45.5: 48.5] cm, ending with RS facing for next row.
Shape armholes
Cast off 3 [3: 4: 4: 5] sts at beg of next 2 rows. 73 [79: 83: 91: 97] sts.
Dec 1 st at each end of next 3 [3: 3: 5: 5] rows, then on foll 3 [4: 4: 4: 4] alt rows. 61 [65: 69: 73: 79] sts.

Cont straight until armhole meas 12.5 [13.5: 14.5: 16: 17] cm, ending with RS facing for next row.
Shape shoulders and back neck
Next row (RS): Cast off 5 [5: 6: 6: 7] sts, K until there are 13 [14: 14: 15: 16] sts on right needle and turn, leaving rem sts on a holder.
Work each side of neck separately.
Dec 1 st at neck edge of next 3 rows, ending with RS facing for next row, **and at same time** cast off 5 [5: 6: 6: 7] sts at beg of 2nd row.
Cast off rem 5 [6: 5: 6: 6] sts.
Return to sts left on holder and slip centre 25 [27: 29: 31: 33] sts onto another holder (for neckband). Rejoin yarn with RS facing and K to end. Complete to match first side, reversing shapings.

FRONT
Work as given for back until 10 [12: 12: 12: 14] rows less have been worked than on back to beg of shoulder shaping, ending with RS facing for next row.

Shape front neck
Next row (RS): K22 [24: 25: 26: 29] and turn, leaving rem sts on a holder.
Work each side of neck separately.
Dec 1 st at neck edge of next 4 rows, then on foll 2 [3: 3: 3: 4] alt rows. 16 [17: 18: 19: 21] sts.

Work 1 row, ending with RS facing for next row.

Shape shoulder

Cast off 5 [5: 6: 6: 7] sts at beg of next and foll alt row **and at same time** dec 1 st at neck edge of next row.

Work 1 row.

Cast off rem 5 [6: 5: 6: 6] sts.

Return to sts left on holder and slip centre 17 [17: 19: 21: 21] sts onto another holder (for neckband). Rejoin yarn with RS facing and K to end. Complete to match first side, reversing shapings.

SLEEVES

Using 3¼mm (US 3) needles cast on 35 [37: 37: 39: 41] sts.

Work in rib as given for back for 8 [8: 10: 10: 10] rows, ending with RS facing for next row.

Change to 3¾mm (US 5) needles.

Beg with a K row, now work in st st throughout as folls:

Inc 1 st at each end of 5th [7th: 5th: 5th: 5th] and 2 [0: 4: 5: 2] foll 6th rows, then on every foll 8th row until there are 49 [53: 57: 63: 67] sts.

Cont straight until sleeve meas 23 [27: 31: 35: 40] cm, ending with RS facing for next row.

Shape top

Cast off 3 [3: 4: 4: 5] sts at beg of next 2 rows. 43 [47: 49: 55: 57] sts.

Dec 1 st at each end of next and foll alt row, then on 2 foll 4th rows. 35 [39: 41: 47: 49] sts.

Work 1 row.

Dec 1 st at each end of next and foll 2 [3: 5: 5: 7] alt rows, then on foll 7 [7: 5: 7: 5] rows, ending with RS facing for next row.

Cast off rem 15 [17: 19: 21: 23] sts.

MAKING UP

Press as described on the information page.

Join both shoulder seams.

Neckband

With RS facing and using 3¼mm (US 3) circular needle, pick up and knit 13 [15: 15: 15: 17] sts down left side of front neck, K across 17 [17: 19: 21: 21] sts on front holder, pick up and knit 13 [15: 15: 15: 17] sts up right side of front neck, and 3 sts down right side of back neck, K across 25 [27: 29: 31: 33] sts on back holder, then pick up and knit 3 sts up left side of back neck. 74 [80: 84: 88: 94] sts. Join to work in rnds, placing marker for beg of rnd.

Round 1 (RS): *K1, P1, rep from * to end.

This round forms rib.

Work in rib for a further 4 rounds.

Cast off **very loosely** in rib, taking care cast-off edge will stretch over child's head.

See information page for finishing instructions, setting in sleeves using the set-in method.

V neck tunic

BACK

Work as given for back of round neck tunic.

FRONT

Work as given for back of round neck tunic until 22 [24: 24: 24: 26] rows less have been worked than on back to beg of shoulder shaping, ending with RS facing for next row.

Shape front neck

Next row (RS): K30 [32: 34: 36: 39] and turn, leaving rem sts on a holder.

Work each side of neck separately.

Dec 1 st at neck edge of next 12 [12: 14: 14: 16] rows, then on foll 3 [4: 3: 4: 3] alt rows. 15 [16: 17: 18: 20] sts.

Work 3 rows, ending with RS facing for next row.

Shape shoulder

Cast off 5 [5: 6: 6: 7] sts at beg of next and foll alt row.

Work 1 row.

Cast off rem 5 [6: 5: 6: 6] sts.

Return to sts left on holder and slip centre st onto another holder (for neckband). Rejoin yarn with RS facing and K to end. 30 [32: 34: 36: 39] sts. Complete to match first side, reversing shapings.

SLEEVES

Work as given for sleeves of round neck tunic.

MAKING UP

Press as described on the information page.

Join both shoulder seams.

Neckband

With RS facing and using 3¼mm (US 3) circular needle, pick up and knit 22 [24: 24: 24: 26] sts down left side of front neck, K st on holder at base of V and mark this st with a coloured thread, pick up and knit 22 [24: 24: 24: 26] sts up right side of front neck, and 3 sts down right side of back neck, K across 25 [27: 29: 31: 33] sts on back holder, then pick up and knit 3 sts up left side of back neck. 76 [82: 84: 86: 92] sts. Join to work in rnds, placing marker for beg of rnd.

Round 1 (RS): *K1, P1, rep from * to end.

This round forms rib.

Keeping rib correct, cont as folls:

Round 2: Rib to within 1 st of marked st, slip next 2 sts as though to K2tog (marked st is second of these 2 sts), K1, then pass 2 slipped sts over, rib to end.

Rep last round 3 times more. 68 [74: 76: 78: 84] sts

Still decreasing 1 st at each side of marked st as before, cast off **very loosely** in rib, taking care cast-off edge will stretch over child's head.

See information page for finishing instructions, setting in sleeves using the set-in method.

v neck

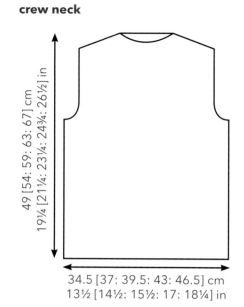

49 [54: 59: 63: 67] cm
19¼ [21¼: 23¼: 24¾: 26½] in

34.5 [37: 39.5: 43: 46.5] cm
13½ [14½: 15½: 17: 18¼] in

crew neck

49 [54: 59: 63: 67] cm
19¼ [21¼: 23¼: 24¾: 26½] in

34.5 [37: 39.5: 43: 46.5] cm
13½ [14½: 15½: 17: 18¼] in

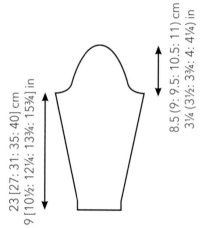

8.5 (9: 9.5: 10.5: 11) cm
3¼ (3½: 3¾: 4: 4¼) in

23 [27: 31: 35: 40] cm
9 [10½: 12¼: 13¾: 15¾] in

Dream
quail studio
★★☆☆

SIZE

To fit age

	3-4	5-6	7-8	9-10	11-12	years
To fit chest						
	53-56	59-61	64-66	69-74	76-79	cm
	21-22	23-24	25-26	27-29	30-31	in
Actual chest measurement of garment						
	73	78	83	93	98	cm
	28½	30½	32½	36½	38½	in

YARN

Rowan Big Wool

5	5	6	6	7	x 100gm

(photographed in Ice Blue 21)

NEEDLES

1 pair 10mm (no 000) (US 15) needles
Cable needle

EXTRAS

Stitch holders
Stitch markers

TENSION

8 sts and 16 rows to 10 cm / 4 in measured over
g st using 10mm (US 15) needles.

BACK

Using 10mm (US 15) needles cast on 29 [31: 33:
37: 39] sts.
Row 1 (RS): K1, *P1, K1, rep from * to end.
Row 2: P1, *K1, P1, rep from * to end.
These 2 rows form rib.
Cont in rib until back meas 4 [4: 5: 5: 5] cm,
ending with RS facing for next row.
Now work in g st throughout as folls:
Cont straight until back meas 40 [44: 48: 52: 55] cm,
ending with RS facing for next row.
Shape shoulders
Cast off 8 [9: 9: 11: 11] sts at beg of next 2 rows.
Break yarn and leave rem 13 [13: 15: 15: 17] sts on
a holder (for neckband).

FRONT

Work as given for back until 8 [8: 8: 8: 10] rows
less have been worked than on back to beg of
shoulder shaping, ending with RS facing for
next row.
Shape front neck
Next row (RS): K12 [13: 13: 15: 16] and turn,
leaving rem sts on a holder.
Work each side of neck separately.
Dec 1 st at neck edge of next 2 rows, then on foll
2 [2: 2: 2: 3] alt rows. 8 [9: 9: 11: 11] sts.

Work 1 row, ending with RS facing for next row.
Shape shoulder
Cast off rem 8 [9: 9: 11: 11] sts.
Return to sts left on holder and slip centre 5 [5:
7: 7: 7] sts onto another holder (for neckband).
Rejoin yarn with RS facing and K to end. Complete
to match first side, reversing shapings.

SLEEVES

Using 10mm (US 15) needles cast on 15 [15: 15:
17: 17] sts.
Cont in rib as given for back for 4 [4: 5: 5: 5] cm,
ending with **WS** facing for next row.
Next row (WS): Rib 5 [5: 5: 6: 6], (inc in next st, rib
1) twice, inc in next st, rib 5 [5: 5: 6: 6]. 18 [18: 18:
20: 20] sts.
Now work in patt as folls:
Row 1 (RS): K5 [5: 5: 6: 6], slip next 4 sts onto
cable needle and leave at back of work, K4, then
K4 from cable needle, K5 [5: 5: 6: 6].
Row 2: K5 [5: 5: 6: 6], P8, K5 [5: 5: 6: 6].
Row 3: Knit.
Rows 4 and 5: As rows 2 and 3.
Row 6: As row 2.
These 6 rows form patt.
Cont in patt, shaping sides by inc 1 st at each end
of 7th [3rd: next: 3rd: 3rd] and every foll 14th
[12th: 10th: 10th: 10th] row to 22 [24: 26: 24: 28] sts,
then on every foll - [-: -: 12th: 12th] row until there
are - [-: -: 28: 30] sts, taking inc sts into g st.
Cont straight until sleeve meas 25 [29: 33: 37: 42] cm,
ending with RS facing for next row.
Cast off.

MAKING UP

Press as described on the information page.
Join right shoulder seam.

Neckband

With RS facing and using 10mm (US 15) needles, pick up and knit 7 [7: 7: 9: 9] sts down left side of front neck, K across 5 [5: 7: 7: 7] sts on front holder, pick up and knit 7 [7: 7: 9: 9] sts up right side of front neck, and then K across 13 [13: 15: 15: 17] sts on back holder inc 1 st at centre. 33 [33: 37: 41: 43] sts.

Beg with row 2, work in rib as given for back for 4 [4: 5: 5: 5] cm, ending with RS facing for next row.
Cast off **very loosely** in rib, making sure cast-off edge will stretch over child's head.

Join left shoulder and neckband seam. Mark points along side seam edges 13 [14: 15: 16.5: 18] cm either side of shoulder seams (to denote base of armhole openings). See information page for finishing instructions, setting in sleeves using the straight cast-off method.

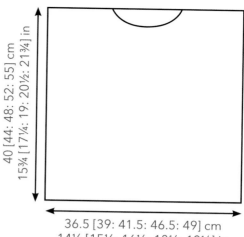
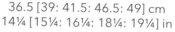

40 [44: 48: 52: 55] cm
15¾ [17¼: 19: 20½: 21¾] in

36.5 [39: 41.5: 46.5: 49] cm
14¼ [15¼: 16¼: 18¼: 19¼] in

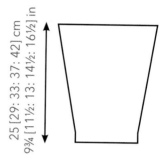

25 [29: 33: 37: 42] cm
9¾ [11½: 13: 14½: 16½] in

quail studio

★★☆☆

SIZE
To fit age

	3-7	9-12	years
Width around head (unstretched)			
	37	41	cm
	14½	16¼	in

YARN
Rowan Alpaca Soft DK

	2	2	x 50gm

(photographed in Rainy Day 210 & Simply White 201)

NEEDLES
1 pair 6mm (no 4) (US 10) needles

EXTRAS - Rowan faux fur pom pom

TENSION
20 sts and 22 rows to 10 cm / 4 in measured over rib using 6mm (US 10) needles and yarn DOUBLE.

HAT
Using 6mm (US 10) needles and yarn DOUBLE cast on 74 [82] sts.
Row 1 (RS): K2, *P2, K2, rep from * to end.
Row 2: P2, *K2, P2, rep from * to end.
These 2 rows form rib.
Cont in rib until hat meas 17 [18] cm, ending with RS facing for next row.
Shape top
Row 1 (RS): K2, (P2, K2, P2tog, K2) 9 [10] times. 65 [72] sts.
Row 2: (P2, K1, P2, K2) 9 [10] times, P2.
Row 3: K2, (P2, K2, P1, K2) 9 [10] times.
Row 4: As row 2.
Row 5: K2, (P2tog, K2, P1, K2) 9 [10] times. 56 [62] sts.
Row 6: (P2, K1) 18 [20] times, P2.
Row 7: K2, (P1, K2) 18 [20] times.
Row 8: As row 6.
Row 9: K2, (P1, K2tog, P1, K2) 9 [10] times. 47 [52] sts.
Row 10: (P2, K1, P1, K1) 9 [10] times, P2.
Row 11: K2tog, (P1, K1, P1, K2tog) 9 [10] times. 37 [41] sts.
Row 12: P1, *K1, P1, rep from * to end.
Row 13: K1, (P1, sl 1, K1, psso, K1) 9 [10] times. 28 [31] sts.
Row 14: (P2, K1) 9 [10] times, P1.
Row 15: (Sl 1, K1, psso, K1) 9 [10] times, K1. 19 [21] sts.

Row 16: (P2tog) 9 [10] times, P1.
Break yarn and thread through rem 10 [11] sts.
Pull up tight and fasten off securely.

MAKING UP
Press as described on the information page.
Join back seam, reversing seam for 3 cm turn back.
If desired, attach pompom to top of hat. See information page for finishing instructions.

Tallulah

georgia farrell

★ ★ ★ ☆

SIZE
To fit age

3-7	9-12	years

YARN
Rowan Alpaca Soft DK

4	5	x 50gm

(photographed in Rainy Day 210)

NEEDLES
Set of 4 double-pointed 3¾mm (no 9) (US 5) needles
Set of 4 double-pointed 4mm (no 8) (US 6) needles

EXTRAS
2 Rowan faux fur pom poms
Stitch marker

TENSION
19 sts and 48 rounds to 10 cm measured over patt using 4mm (US 6) needles.

FINISHED SIZE
Completed scarf is 12 [15] cm (4¾ [6] in) wide and 115 [125] cm (45¼ [49¼] in) long, excluding pompoms.

SPECIAL ABBREVIATIONS
K1 below = K into next st one row below and at same time slipping off st above; **P1 below** = P into next st one row below and at same time slipping off st above.

SCARF
Using double-pointed 3¾mm (US 5) needles cast on 46 [58] sts.
Distribute sts evenly over 3 of the 4 needles and, using 4th needle and taking care not to twist cast-on edge, place marker work in rounds as folls:
Round 1 (RS): *K1, P1, rep from * to end.
This round forms rib.
Work in rib until scarf meas 3 [4] cm.
Change to double-pointed 4mm (US 6) needles.
Now work in patt as folls:

Round 1: *K1, P1 below (see special abbreviations), rep from * to end.
Round 2: *K1 below (see special abbreviations), P1, rep from * to end.
These 2 rounds form patt.
Cont in patt until scarf meas 112 [121] cm.
Change to double-pointed 3¾mm (US 5) needles.
Work in rib as given for cast-on edge for 3 [4] cm.
Cast off in rib.

MAKING UP
Press as described on the information page.
Run gathering threads around cast-on and cast-off edges, pull up tight and then attach pompoms to gathered ends of scarf. See information page for finishing instructions.

Fifi

quail studio

★ ☆ ☆ ☆

SIZE
To fit age

3-7	9-12	years

YARN
Rowan Soft Bouclé
Fringed scarf

2	2	x 50gm

(photographed in Snow)

NEEDLES
1 pair 6mm (no 4) (US 10) needles

TENSION
12½ sts and 17 rows to 10 cm / 4 in measured over st st using 6mm (US 10) needles.

FINISHED SIZE
Completed scarf is 12 [14.5] cm (4¾ [5¾] in) wide and 170 [200] cm (67 [78¾] in) long, excluding fringe.

SCARF
Using 6mm (US 10) needles cast on 15 [18] sts.
Beg with a K row, work in st st until scarf meas 170 [200] cm, ending with RS facing for next row.
Cast off.

MAKING UP
Press as described on the information page.
For fringed scarf, cut 25 [32] cm lengths of yarn and knot groups of 6 of these lengths through cast-on and cast-off edge to form fringe – position 6 [7] knots evenly spaced along edge.
See information page for finishing instructions.

Teddy

quail studio

★ ★ ☆ ☆

SIZE

To fit age	3-4	5-6	7-8	9-10	11-12	years
To fit chest						
	53-56	59-61	64-66	69-74	76-79	cm
	21-22	23-24	25-26	27-29	30-31	in
Actual chest measurement of garment						
	75	80	85	95	100	cm
	29½	31½	33½	37½	39½	in

YARN

Rowan Soft Bouclé

	6	6	7	7	8	x 50gm

(photographed in Biscuit 608 & Snow 600)

NEEDLES

1 pair 12mm (US 17) needles

TENSION

8 sts and 12½ rows to 10 cm / 4 in measured over rev st st using 12mm (US 17) needles and yarn DOUBLE.

BACK

Using 12mm (US 17) needles and yarn DOUBLE cast on 30 [32: 34: 38: 40] sts.
Beg with a P row, now work in rev st st throughout as folls:
Cont straight until back meas 53 [58: 63: 68: 72] cm, ending with RS facing for next row.

Shape shoulders

Cast off 10 [10: 11: 12: 13] sts at beg of next 2 rows.
Cast off rem 10 [12: 12: 14: 14] sts.

LEFT FRONT

Using 12mm (US 17) needles and yarn DOUBLE cast on 20 [22: 23: 26: 27] sts.
Row 1 (RS): P to last 4 sts, K4.
Row 2: Knit.
These 2 rows set the sts – front opening edge 4 sts in g st with all other sts in rev st st.
Cont as set until left front matches back to shoulder shaping, ending with RS facing for next row.

Shape shoulder

Cast off 10 [10: 11: 12: 13] sts at beg of next row.
Cont on rem 10 [12: 12: 14: 14] sts only (for back neck border extension) until this strip meas 6 [7.5: 7.5: 9: 9] cm, ending with RS facing for next row.
Cast off.

RIGHT FRONT

Using 12mm (US 17) needles and yarn DOUBLE cast on 20 [22: 23: 26: 27] sts.
Row 1 (RS): K4, P to end.
Row 2: Knit.
These 2 rows set the sts – front opening edge 4 sts in g st with all other sts in rev st st.
Keeping sts correct throughout, complete to match left front, reversing shapings.

SLEEVES

Using 12mm (US 17) needles and yarn DOUBLE cast on 16 [18: 18: 20: 20] sts.
Beg with a P row, now work in rev st st throughout as folls:
Inc 1 st at each end of 11th [15th: 11th: 11th: 9th] and every foll 14th [16th: 12th: 14th: 12th] row until there are 20 [22: 24: 26: 28] sts.
Cont straight until sleeve meas 25 [29: 33: 37: 42] cm, ending with RS facing for next row.
Cast off.

MAKING UP

Press as described on the information page. Join both shoulder seams. Join cast-off ends of back neck border extensions, then sew one edge to back neck. Mark points along side seam edges 13 [14: 15: 16.5: 18] cm either side of shoulder seams (to denote base of armhole openings). See information page for finishing instructions, setting in sleeves using the straight cast-off method.

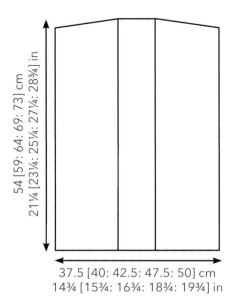

54 [59: 64: 69: 73] cm
21¼ [23¼: 25¼: 27¼: 28¾] in

37.5 [40: 42.5: 47.5: 50] cm
14¾ [15¾: 16¾: 18¾: 19¾] in

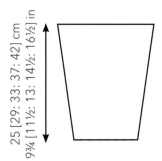

25 [29: 33: 37: 42] cm
9¾ [11½: 13: 14½: 16½] in

Luna

martin storey

★ ★ ★ ☆

SIZE

To fit age						
	3-4	5-6	7-8	9-10	11-12	years
To fit chest						
	53-56	59-61	64-66	69-74	76-79	cm
	21-22	23-24	25-26	27-29	30-31	in
Actual chest measurement of garment						
	69	77	81	87	94	cm
	27	30½	32	34½	36¾	in

YARN

Rowan Cotton Cashmere

	6	6	7	7	8	x 50gm

(photographed in Pearly Pink 216)

NEEDLES

1 pair 3¼mm (no 10) (US 3) needles
1 pair 3¾mm (no 9) (US 5) needles
Cable needle

EXTRAS

Stitch holders
Stitch markers

TENSION

31 sts and 34 rows to 10 cm / 4 in measured over patt using 3¾mm (US 5) needles.

SPECIAL ABBREVIATIONS

C6B = slip next 3 sts onto cable needle and leave at back of work, K3, then K3 from cable needle;
C6F = slip next 3 sts onto cable needle and leave at front of work, K3, then K3 from cable needle;
MB = make bobble as folls: (K1, yfwd, K1, yfwd, K1) all into next st, turn, P5, turn, K5, turn, sl 1, K1, psso, K1, K2tog, turn, P3tog and, keeping yarn at WS of work, slip bobble st onto right needle.

BACK

Using 3¼mm (US 3) needles cast on 107 [119: 125: 135: 145] sts.
Beg and ending rows as indicated and repeating the 22 st patt repeat 4 [4: 5: 5: 5] times across each row, cont in patt from chart for body as folls:
Work chart rows 1 and 2, 7 [7: 8: 8: 8] times, ending with RS facing for next row.
These 14 [14: 16: 16: 16] rows complete rib.
Change to 3¾mm (US 5) needles.

Now repeating chart rows 3 to 18 **throughout**, cont as folls:
Cont straight until back meas 37 [41: 45: 49: 52] cm, ending with RS facing for next row.
Shape shoulders
Keeping patt correct, cast off 3 [4: 4: 4: 5] sts at beg of next 2 [12: 8: 2: 12] rows, then 4 [5: 5: 5: 6] sts at beg of foll 16 [6: 10: 16: 6] rows.
Break yarn and leave rem 37 [41: 43: 47: 49] sts on a holder (for neckband).

FRONT

Work as given for back until 4 [6: 6: 6: 8] rows less have been worked than on back to beg of shoulder shaping, ending with RS facing for next row.
Shape front neck
Next row (RS): Patt 45 [50: 52: 55: 60] sts and turn, leaving rem sts on a holder.
Work each side of neck separately.
Keeping patt correct, dec 1 st at neck edge of next 3 [5: 5: 5: 6] rows. 42 [45: 47: 50: 54] sts.
Work - [-: -: -: 1] row, ending with RS facing for next row.

Shape shoulder

Keeping patt correct, cast off 3 [4: 4: 4: 5] sts at beg of next and foll - [5: 3: -: 5] alt rows, then 4 [5: 5: 5: 6] sts at beg of foll 7 [2: 4: 7: 2] alt rows **and at same time** dec 1 st at neck edge of next 3 [1: 1: 1: 1] rows, then on foll 3 [4: 4: 4: 4] alt rows, then on foll 4th row.

Work 1 row.

Cast off rem 4 [5: 5: 5: 6] sts.

Return to sts left on holder and slip centre 17 [19: 21: 25: 25] sts onto another holder (for neckband).

Rejoin yarn with RS facing and patt to end.

Complete to match first side, reversing shapings.

SLEEVES

Using 3¼mm (US 3) needles cast on 51 [55: 55: 59: 59] sts.

Beg and ending rows as indicated, cont in patt from chart for sleeve as folls:

Work chart rows 1 and 2, 7 [7: 8: 8: 8] times, ending with RS facing for next row.

These 14 [14: 16: 16: 16] rows complete rib.

Change to 3¾mm (US 5) needles.

Now repeating chart rows 3 to 18 **throughout**, cont as folls:

Inc 1 st at each end of 3rd and every foll 4th row until there are 75 [69: 87: 97: 105] sts, then on - [5: -: -: -] foll 6th rows, taking inc sts into patt. 75 [79: 87: 97: 105] sts.

Cont straight until sleeve meas 22 [25: 29: 32: 37] cm, ending with RS facing for next row.

Cast off.

MAKING UP

Press as described on the information page.

Join right shoulder seam.

Neckband

With RS facing and using 3¼mm (US 3) needles, pick up and knit 17 [18: 18: 18: 21] sts down left side of front neck, K across 17 [19: 21: 25: 25] sts on front holder dec 3 sts evenly, pick up and knit 17 [18: 18: 18: 21] sts up right side of front neck, then K across 37 [41: 43: 47: 49] sts on back holder dec 3 sts evenly. 82 [90: 94: 102: 110] sts.

Row 1 (WS): P2, *K2, P2, rep from * to end.

Row 2: K2, *P2, K2, rep from * to end.

These 2 rows form rib.

Cont in rib for a further 5 rows, ending with RS facing for next row.

Cast off **very loosely** in rib, taking care cast-off edge will stretch over child's head.

Join left shoulder and neckband seam. Mark points along side seam edges 12 [13: 14: 16.5: 18] cm either side of shoulder seams (to denote base of armhole openings). See information page for finishing instructions, setting in sleeves using the straight cast-off method.

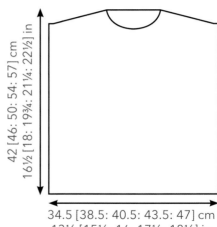

42 [46: 50: 54: 57] cm
16½ [18: 19¾: 21¼: 22½] in

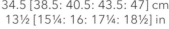

34.5 [38.5: 40.5: 43.5: 47] cm
13½ [15¼: 16: 17¼: 18½] in

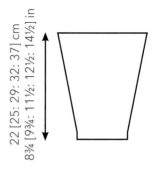

22 [25: 29: 32: 37] cm
8¾ [9¾: 11½: 12½: 14½] in

Luna Cable Sweater Body Chart

Key

- ☐ K on RS rows, P on WS rows
- ● P on RS rows, K on WS rows
- Ⓞ yrn
- ╱ K2tog on WS rows
- ⊡ MB
- ⤫ C6F
- ⤫ C6B

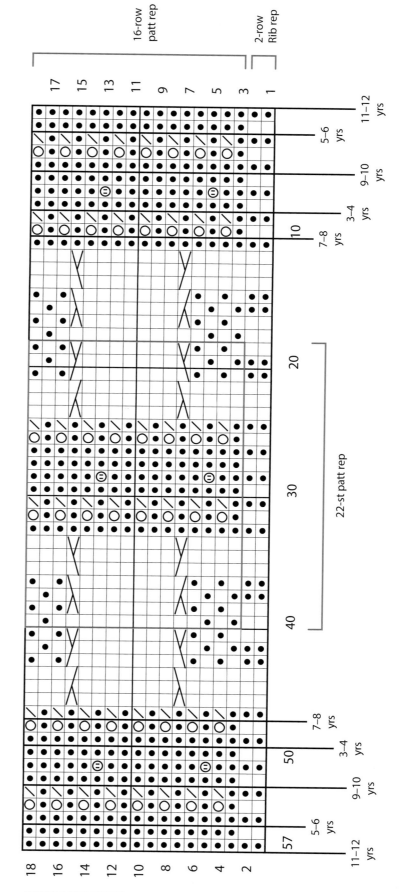

Luna Cable Sweater
Sleeve Chart

Key

- ☐ K on RS rows, P on WS rows
- ● P on RS rows, K on WS rows
- Ⓞ yrn
- ⟋ K2tog on WS rows
- ⊡ MB
- C6F
- C6B

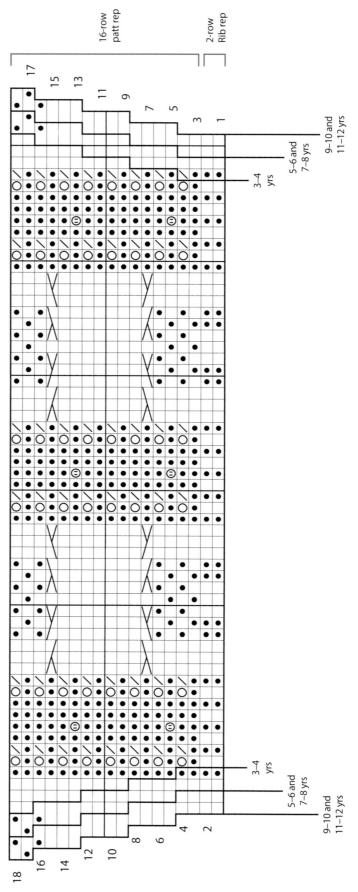

Silver

annika andrea wolke

★ ★ ☆ ☆

SIZE

To fit age						
	3-4	5-6	7-8	9-10	11-12	years
To fit chest						
	53-56	59-61	64-66	69-74	76-79	cm
	21-22	23-24	25-26	27-29	30-31	in
Actual chest measurement of garment						
	81	89	94	101	109	cm
	32	35	37	40	43	in

YARN

Rowan Alpaca Soft DK and Alpaca Classic

A Alpaca Soft DK | Rainy Day 210						
	5	5	6	7	8	x 50gm
B Alpaca Classic | Feather Grey Melange 101						
	5	5	6	7	8	x 25gm

NEEDLES

1 pair 5mm (no 6) (US 8) needles
1 pair 6mm (no 4) (US 10) needles

EXTRAS
Stitch holder

TENSION
16 sts and 22½ rows to 10 cm / 4 in measured over st st using 6mm (US 10) needles and one strand each of yarns A and B held together.

BACK
Using 5mm (US 8) needles and one strand each of yarns A and B held together cast on 65 [71: 75: 81: 87] sts.
Row 1 (RS): K1, *P1, K1, rep from * to end.
Row 2: P1, *K1, P1, rep from * to end.
These 2 rows form rib.
Cont in rib for a further 6 [6: 8: 8: 8] rows, ending with RS facing for next row.
Change to 6mm (US 10) needles.
Beg with a K row, now work in st st throughout as folls:
Cont straight until back meas 45 [50: 55: 58.5: 62] cm, ending with RS facing for next row.
Shape armholes
Cast off 4 [4: 5: 5: 6] sts at beg of next 2 rows. 57 [63: 65: 71: 75] sts.
Dec 1 st at each end of next 5 rows, then on foll 3 [5: 5: 6: 6] alt rows. 41 [43: 45: 49: 53] sts.

Cont straight until armhole meas 13 [14: 15: 16.5: 18] cm, ending with RS facing for next row.
Shape shoulders and back neck
Next row (RS): Cast off 5 [5: 5: 6: 7] sts, K until there are 9 [9: 9: 9: 10] sts on right needle and turn, leaving rem sts on a holder.
Work each side of neck separately.
Cast off 3 sts at beg of next row.
Cast off rem 6 [6: 6: 6: 7] sts.
Return to sts left on holder and rejoin yarns with RS facing. Cast off centre 13 [15: 17: 19: 19] sts at beg of next row. Complete to match first side, reversing shapings.

LEFT FRONT
Using 5mm (US 8) needles and one strand each of yarns A and B held together cast on 32 [34: 34: 36: 40] sts.
Row 1 (RS): *K1, P1, rep from * to last 2 sts, K2.
Row 2: *K1, P1, rep from * to end.
These 2 rows form rib.
Cont in rib for a further 6 [6: 8: 8: 8] rows, inc 0 [0: 1: 1: 0] st at end of last row and ending with RS facing for next row. 32 [34: 35: 37: 40] sts.
Change to 6mm (US 10) needles.
Next row (RS): K to last 9 sts, (P1, K1) 4 times, K1.
Next row: K1, (P1, K1) 4 times, P to end.

Last 2 rows set the sts – front opening edge 9 sts still in rib with all other sts now in st st.
Keeping sts correct throughout, cont as folls:
Cont straight until left front matches back to beg of armhole shaping, ending with RS facing for next row.

Shape armhole
Cast off 4 [4: 5: 5: 6] sts at beg of next row. 28 [30: 30: 32: 34] sts.
Work 1 row.
Dec 1 st at armhole edge of next 5 rows, then on foll 3 [5: 5: 6: 6] alt rows. 20 [20: 20: 21: 23] sts.
Cont straight until left front matches back to beg of shoulder shaping, ending with RS facing for next row.

Shape shoulder
Cast off 5 [5: 5: 6: 7] sts at beg of next row, then 6 [6: 6: 6: 7] sts at beg of foll alt row. 9 sts.
Work 1 row, inc 1 st at end of next row. 10 sts.
Working first and last st of every row as a K st and all other sts in rib as set, cont on these 10 sts only (for back neck border extension) until this strip meas 6 [6.5: 7: 7.5: 7.5] cm, ending with RS facing for next row.
Cast off.

RIGHT FRONT
Using 5mm (US 8) needles and one strand each of yarns A and B held together cast on 32 [34: 34: 36: 40] sts.
Row 1 (RS): K2, *P1, K1, rep from * to end.
Row 2: *P1, K1, rep from * to end.
These 2 rows form rib.
Cont in rib for a further 6 [6: 8: 8: 8] rows, inc 0 [0: 1: 1: 0] st at beg of last row and ending with RS facing for next row. 32 [34: 35: 37: 40] sts.
Change to 6mm (US 10) needles.
Next row (RS): K1, (K1, P1) 4 times, K to end.
Next row: P to last 9 sts, (K1, P1) 4 times, K1.
Last 2 rows set the sts – front opening edge 9 sts still in rib with all other sts now in st st.
Keeping sts correct throughout, complete to match left front, reversing shapings.

SLEEVES
Using 5mm (US 8) needles and one strand each of yarns A and B held together cast on 29 [31: 31: 33: 33] sts.
Work in rib as given for back for 8 [8: 10: 10: 10] rows, ending with RS facing for next row.
Change to 6mm (US 10) needles.
Beg with a K row, now work in st st throughout as folls:
Inc 1 st at each end of 9th [9th: 7th: 7th: 7th] and every foll 10th [12th: 8th: 8th: 8th] row to 37 [39: 41: 43: 51] sts, then on every foll – [-: 10th: 10th: -] row until there are - [-: 43: 47: -] sts.

Cont straight until sleeve meas 24 [28: 32: 36: 41] cm, ending with RS facing for next row.

Shape top
Cast off 4 [4: 5: 5: 6] sts at beg of next 2 rows. 29 [31: 33: 37: 39] sts.
Dec 1 st at each end of next and foll 2 alt rows, then on foll 4th row. 21 [23: 25: 29: 31] sts.
Work 1 row.
Dec 1 st at each end of next and foll 2 [1: 2: 2: 3] alt rows, then on foll 3 [5: 5: 7: 7] rows, ending with RS facing for next row.
Cast off rem 9 sts.

MAKING UP
Press as described on the information page.
Join both shoulder seams. Join cast-off ends of back neck border extensions, then sew one edge to back neck.
See information page for finishing instructions, setting in sleeves using the set-in method.

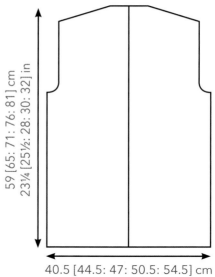

59 [65: 71: 76: 81] cm
23¼ [25½: 28: 30: 32] in

40.5 [44.5: 47: 50.5: 54.5] cm
16 [17½: 18½: 20: 21½] in

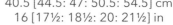

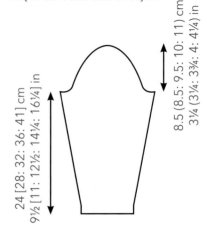

8.5 (8.5: 9.5: 10: 11) cm
3¼ (3¼: 3¾: 4: 4¼) in

24 [28: 32: 36: 41] cm
9½ [11: 12½: 14¼: 16¼] in

Moon
lisa richardson
★ ★ ☆ ☆

SIZE

To fit age				
	3-6	7-9	10-12	years
To fit chest				
	53-61	64-69	74-79	cm
	21-24	25-27	29-31	in
Actual chest measurement of garment				
	64	73	82.5	cm
	25¼	28¾	32½	in

YARN
Rowan Alpaca Soft DK and Alpaca Classic

A Alpaca Soft DK	Simply White 201			
	3	4	5	x 50gm
B Alpaca Classic	Snowflake White 115			
	3	4	5	x 25gm

NEEDLES
1 pair 7mm (no 2) (US 10½/11) needles

TENSION
13 sts and 25 rows to 10 cm measured over moss
st using 7mm (US 10½/11) needles and one strand
each of yarns A and B held together.

PONCHO
Using 7mm (US 10½/11) needles and one strand
each of yarns A and B held together cast on
83 [95: 107] sts.
Row 1 (RS): K1, *P1, K1, rep from * to end.
Row 2: As row 1.
These 2 rows form moss st.
Cont in moss st until work meas 30 [34: 38] cm,
ending with RS facing for next row.
Shape neck opening
Next row (RS): Moss st 27 [32: 37] sts, cast off next
29 [31: 33] sts in moss st, moss st to end.
Next row: Moss st 27 [32: 37] sts, turn and cast on
29 [31: 33] sts, turn and moss st to end.
Cont straight until work meas 30 [34: 38] cm from
neck opening, ending with RS facing for next row.
Cast off in moss st.

MAKING UP
Press as described on the information page.
See information page for finishing instructions.

Alaska
quail studio
★★☆☆

SIZE

To fit age						
	3-4	5-6	7-8	9-10	11-12	years
To fit chest						
	53-56	59-61	64-66	69-74	76-79	cm
	21-22	23-24	25-26	27-29	30-31	in
Actual chest measurement of garment						
	75	82	88	95	102	cm
	29½	32½	34½	37½	20	in

YARN

Rowan Alpaca Classic

	9	9	10	11	11	x 25gm

(photographed in Iced Blue 131)

NEEDLES

1 pair 5mm (no 6) (US 8) needles
1 pair 6mm (no 4) (US 10) needles

EXTRAS

Stitch holders

TENSION

18 sts and 26 rows to 10 cm / 4 in measured over g st using 6mm (US 10) needles and yarn DOUBLE. Lace panel (23 sts) measures 12 cm.

BACK

Using 5mm (US 8) needles and yarn DOUBLE cast on 69 [75: 81: 87: 93] sts.
Row 1 (RS): K1, *P1, K1, rep from * to end.
Row 2: P1, *K1, P1, rep from * to end.
These 2 rows form rib.
Cont in rib for a further 6 [6: 6: 8: 8] rows, ending with RS facing for next row.
Change to 6mm (US 10) needles.
Now work in patt as folls:
Row 1 (RS): K8 [10: 13: 15: 18], *K8, K2tog, yfwd, K1, P1, K1, yfwd, sl 1, K1, psso, K8*, K7 [9: 9: 11: 11], rep from * to * once more, K8 [10: 13: 15: 18].
Row 2: K8 [10: 13: 15: 18], *P7, P2tog tbl, P2, yon, K1, yfrn, P2, P2tog, P7*, K7 [9: 9: 11: 11], rep from * to * once more, K8 [10: 13: 15: 18].
Row 3: K8 [10: 13: 15: 18], *K6, K2tog, K1, yfwd, K2, P1, K2, yfwd, K1, sl 1, K1, psso, K6*, K7 [9: 9: 11: 11], rep from * to * once more, K8 [10: 13: 15: 18].
Row 4: K8 [10: 13: 15: 18], *P5, P2tog tbl, P3, yrn, P1, K1, P1, yrn, P3, P2tog, P5*, K7 [9: 9: 11: 11], rep from * to * once more, K8 [10: 13: 15: 18].
Row 5: K8 [10: 13: 15: 18], *K4, K2tog, K2, yfwd, K3,

P1, K3, yfwd, K2, sl 1, K1, psso, K4*, K7 [9: 9: 11: 11], rep from * to * once more, K8 [10: 13: 15: 18].
Row 6: K8 [10: 13: 15: 18], *P3, P2tog tbl, P4, yrn, P2, K1, P2, yrn, P4, P2tog, P3*, K7 [9: 9: 11: 11], rep from * to * once more, K8 [10: 13: 15: 18].
Row 7: K8 [10: 13: 15: 18], *K2, K2tog, K3, yfwd, K4, P1, K4, yfwd, K3, sl 1, K1, psso, K2*, K7 [9: 9: 11: 11], rep from * to * once more, K8 [10: 13: 15: 18].
Row 8: K8 [10: 13: 15: 18], *P1, P2tog tbl, P5, yrn, P3, K1, P3, yrn, P5, P2tog, P1*, K7 [9: 9: 11: 11], rep from * to * once more, K8 [10: 13: 15: 18].
Row 9: K8 [10: 13: 15: 18], *K2tog, K4, yfwd, K5, P1, K5, yfwd, K4, sl 1, K1, psso*, K7 [9: 9: 11: 11], rep from * to * once more, K8 [10: 13: 15: 18].
Row 10: K8 [10: 13: 15: 18], *P11, K1, P11*, K7 [9: 9: 11: 11], rep from * to * once more, K8 [10: 13: 15: 18].
Row 11: K8 [10: 13: 15: 18], *K11, P1, K11*, K7 [9: 9: 11: 11], rep from * to * once more, K8 [10: 13: 15: 18].
Row 12: As row 10.
These 12 rows form patt – 2 lace panels with g st between and at sides.
Cont in patt until back meas 28 [31: 34: 36.5: 41] cm, ending with RS facing for next row.

Shape armholes

Keeping patt correct, cast off 2 sts at beg of next 2 rows. 65 [71: 77: 83: 89] sts.
Next row (RS): K2, sl 1, K1, psso, patt to last 4 sts, K2tog, K2. 63 [69: 75: 81: 87] sts.

Working all armhole decreases as set by last row, dec 1 st at each end of 2nd and foll alt row. 59 [65: 71: 77: 83] sts.

Cont straight until armhole meas 13 [14: 15: 16.5: 18] cm, ending with RS facing for next row.

Shape shoulders and back neck
Next row (RS): Cast off 8 [9: 10: 11: 12] sts, patt until there are 12 [13: 14: 15: 16] sts on right needle and turn, leaving rem sts on a holder.
Work each side of neck separately.
Cast off 3 sts at beg of next row.
Cast off rem 9 [10: 11: 12: 13] sts.
Return to sts left on holder and slip centre 19 [21: 23: 25: 27] sts onto another holder (for neckband).
Rejoin yarn with RS facing and patt to end.
Complete to match first side, reversing shapings.

FRONT
Work as given for back until 14 [16: 16: 16: 18] rows less have been worked than on back to beg of shoulder shaping, ending with RS facing for next row.

Shape front neck
Next row (RS): Patt 24 [27: 29: 31: 34] sts and turn, leaving rem sts on a holder.
Work each side of neck separately.
Keeping patt correct, dec 1 st at neck edge of next 4 rows, then on foll 2 [3: 3: 3: 4] alt rows, then on foll 4th row. 17 [19: 21: 23: 25] sts.
Work 1 row, ending with RS facing for next row.

Shape shoulder
Cast off 8 [9: 10: 11: 12] sts at beg of next row.
Work 1 row.
Cast off rem 9 [10: 11: 12: 13] sts.
Return to sts left on holder and slip centre 11 [11: 13: 15: 15] sts onto another holder (for neckband).
Rejoin yarn with RS facing and patt to end.
Complete to match first side, reversing shapings.

SLEEVES
Using 5mm (US 8) needles and yarn DOUBLE cast on 23 [25: 25: 27: 27] sts.
Work in rib as given for back for 7 [7: 7: 9: 9] rows, ending with **WS** facing for next row.
Next row (WS): P1, *inc knitwise in next st, P1, rep from * to end. 34 [37: 37: 40: 40] sts.
Change to 6mm (US 10) needles.
Working in g st throughout, cont as folls:
Inc 1 st at each end of 7th [9th: 7th: 7th: 5th] and every foll 8th [10th: 8th: 8th: 6th] row to 40 [43: 41: 50: 44] sts, then on every foll 10th [12th: 10th: 10th: 8th] row until there are 44 [47: 51: 56: 62] sts.
Cont straight until sleeve meas 24 [28: 32: 36: 41] cm, ending with RS facing for next row.

Shape top
Cast off 2 sts at beg of next 2 rows. 40 [43: 47: 52: 58] sts.
Working all sleeve top decreases in same way as

armhole decreases, dec 1 st at each end of next and foll alt row, then on next row, ending with RS facing for next row.
Cast off rem 34 [37: 41: 46: 52] sts.

MAKING UP
Press as described on the information page.
Join right shoulder seam.
Neckband
With RS facing, using 5mm (US 8) needles and yarn DOUBLE, pick up and knit 14 [16: 16: 16: 18] sts down left side of front neck, K across 11 [11: 13: 15: 15] sts on front holder, pick up and knit 14 [16: 16: 16: 18] sts up right side of front neck, and 3 sts down right side of back neck, K across 19 [21: 23: 25: 27] sts on back holder inc 1 st at centre, then pick up and knit 3 sts up left side of back neck. 65 [71: 75: 79: 85] sts.
Beg with row 2, work in rib as given for back for 6 [6: 7: 7: 7] cm, ending with RS facing for next row.
Cast off **very loosely** in rib, taking care cast-off edge will stretch over child's head.
Join left shoulder and neckband seam. Fold neckband in half to inside and loosely sew in place, again taking care to ensure edge will stretch to fit over child's head. See information page for finishing instructions, setting in sleeves using the shallow set-in method.

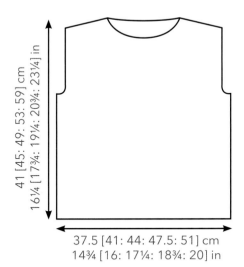

37.5 [41: 44: 47.5: 51] cm
14¾ [16: 17¼: 18¾: 20] in

41 [45: 49: 53: 59] cm
16¼ [17¾: 19¼: 20¾: 23¼] in

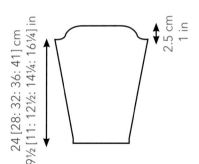

2.5 cm
1 in

24 [28: 32: 36: 41] cm
9½ [11: 12½: 14¼: 16¼] in

Bear

quail studio

★ ★ ☆ ☆

SIZE

To fit age						
	3-4	5-6	7-8	9-10	11-12	years
To fit chest						
	53-56	59-61	64-66	69-74	76-79	cm
	21-22	23-24	25-26	27-29	30-31	in
Actual chest measurement of garment						
	75	82	88	95	102	cm
	29½	32	34½	37½	40	in

YARN

Rowan Soft Bouclé

3	3	4	4	4	x 50gm

(photographed in Shrimp 601 & Natural 602)

NEEDLES

1 pair 6mm (no 4) (US 10) needles

EXTRAS

Stitch markers

TENSION

12 sts and 18 rows to 10 cm / 4 in measured over moss st using 6mm (US 10) needles.

BACK

Using 6mm (US 10) needles cast on 45 [49: 53: 57: 61] sts.
Row 1 (RS): K1, *P1, K1, rep from * to end.
Row 2: As row 1.
These 2 rows form moss st.
Working in moss st throughout, cont as folls:
Cont straight until back meas 39 [44: 48: 52: 54] cm, ending with RS facing for next row.
Shape armholes
Cast off 2 [3: 3: 4: 4] sts at beg of next 2 rows. 41 [43: 47: 49: 53] sts.
Dec 1 st at each end of next 3 rows, then on foll 2 [2: 3: 3: 4] alt rows. 31 [33: 35: 37: 39] sts.
Cont straight until armhole meas 15 [16: 17: 19: 21] cm, ending with RS facing for next row.
Shape shoulders
Cast off 3 [4: 4: 4: 4] sts at beg of next 2 rows, then 4 [4: 4: 4: 5] sts at beg of foll 2 rows.
Cast off rem 17 [17: 19: 21: 21] sts.

LEFT FRONT

Using 6mm (US 10) needles cast on 27 [29: 31: 33: 35] sts.
Working in moss st as given for back throughout, cont as folls:
Cont straight until left front matches back to beg of armhole shaping, ending with RS facing for next row.
Shape armhole
Cast off 2 [3: 3: 4: 4] sts at beg of next row. 25 [26: 28: 29: 31] sts.
Work 1 row.
Shape front slope
Place a marker after 4th st in from front opening edge – this marker denotes fold line for facing.
Next row (RS): Work 2 tog (for armhole dec), moss st to within 2 sts of marker, work 2 tog (for front slope dec of front), slip marker onto right needle, work 2 tog (for front slope dec of facing), moss st 1 st, inc in last st (this inc compensates for facing dec after marker, so facing always has 4 sts beyond marker). 23 [24: 26: 27: 29] sts.
Working all front slope decreases (and facing shaping) as set by last row, cont as folls:
Dec 1 st at armhole edge of next 2 rows, then on foll 2 [2: 3: 3: 4] alt rows **and at same time** dec 1 st at front slope edge of 2nd and foll 2 [2: 3: 3: 4] alt rows. 16 [17: 17: 18: 18] sts.
Dec 1 st at front slope edge **only** on 2nd [2nd: 2nd: 2nd: 4th] and foll 2 [2: 2: 2: 0] alt rows, then on 2 [2: 2: 3: 4] foll 4th rows. 11 [12: 12: 12: 13] sts.
Cont straight until left front matches back to beg of shoulder shaping, ending with RS facing for next row.

Shape shoulder

Cast off 3 [4: 4: 4: 4] sts at beg of next row, then 4 [4: 4: 4: 5] sts at beg of foll alt row. 4 sts.
Work 1 row, inc 1 st at end of next row. 5 sts.
Cont in moss st on these 5 sts only (for back neck facing) until this strip meas 7 [7: 8: 8.5: 8.5] cm, ending with RS facing for next row.
Cast off.

RIGHT FRONT

Using 6mm (US 10) needles cast on 27 [29: 31: 33: 35] sts.
Working in moss st as given for back throughout, cont as folls:
Cont straight until left front matches back to beg of armhole shaping, ending with RS facing for next row.

Shape armhole

Work 1 row.
Cast off 2 [3: 3: 4: 4] sts at beg of next row. 25 [26: 28: 29: 31] sts.

Shape front slope

Place a marker after 4th st in from front opening edge – this marker denotes fold line for facing.
Next row (RS): Inc in first st (this inc compensates for facing dec before marker, so facing always has 4 sts beyond marker), moss st 1 st, work 2 tog (for front slope dec of facing), slip marker onto right needle, work 2 tog (for front slope dec of front), moss st to last 2 sts, work 2 tog (for armhole dec). 23 [24: 26: 27: 29] sts.
Working all front slope decreases (and facing shaping) as set by last row, complete to match left front, reversing shapings.

MAKING UP

Press as described on the information page.
Join both shoulder seams. Join cast-off ends of back neck facing strips, then sew one edge to back neck. Fold 4 sts of facing to inside along front opening and back neck edges and neatly sew in place.
See information page for finishing instructions.

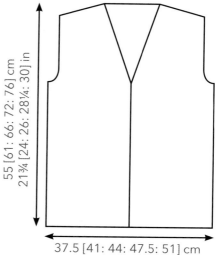

55 [61: 66: 72: 76] cm
21¾ [24: 26: 28¼: 30] in

37.5 [41: 44: 47.5: 51] cm
14¾ [16¼: 17¼: 18¾: 20] in

Ivy

chloe thurlow

★ ★ ☆ ☆

SIZE

To fit age						
	3-4	5-6	7-8	9-10	11-12	years
To fit chest						
	53-56	59-61	64-66	69-74	76-79	cm
	21-22	23-24	25-26	27-29	30-31	in
Actual chest measurement of garment						
	64	70	74	80	86	cm
	25	27½	29	31½	34	in

YARN

Rowan Handknit Cotton
A Iced Water 239

	4	4	5	5	6	x 50gm

B Bleached 263

	1	1	1	1	1	x 50gm

NEEDLES

1 pair 3¼mm (no 10) (US 3) needles
1 pair 4mm (no 8) (US 6) needles
3¼mm (no 10) (US 3) circular needle no more than 50 [50: 60: 70: 70] cm long

EXTRAS

Stitch holders

TENSION

20 sts and 30 rows to 10 cm / 4 in measured over st st using 4mm (US 6) needles.

BACK

Using 3¼mm (US 3) needles and yarn A cast on 63 [69: 73: 79: 85] sts.
Row 1 (RS): K1, *P1, K1, rep from * to end.
Row 2: P1, *K1, P1, rep from * to end.
These 2 rows form rib.
Work in rib for a further 4 [4: 6: 6: 6] rows, inc 1 st at end of last row and ending with RS facing for next row. 64 [70: 74: 80: 86] sts.
Change to 4mm (US 6) needles.
Beg with a K row and joining in yarn B when required, now work in striped st st throughout as folls:
Using yarn A, work 8 [8: 10: 10: 12] rows.
Using yarn B, work 2 rows.
These 10 [10: 12: 12: 14] rows form striped st st.**
Cont in striped st st until back meas 14 [16: 17: 19: 20] cm, ending with RS facing for next row.
Divide for back neck
Next row (RS): K32 [35: 37: 40: 43] and turn, leaving rem sts on a holder.
Work each side of neck separately.
Keeping stripes correct throughout, cont as folls:
Work 1 row.

Next row (RS): K to last 4 sts, K2tog, K2. 31 [34: 36: 39: 42] sts.
Working all back neck decreases as set by last row, dec 1 st at neck edge of 2nd and foll 3 [4: 3: 2: 5] alt rows, then on 11 [12: 14: 16: 15] foll 4th rows. 16 [17: 18: 20: 21] sts.
Work 5 rows, ending with RS facing for next row.
Shape shoulder
Cast off 5 [6: 6: 7: 7] sts at beg of next and foll alt row.
Work 1 row.
Cast off rem 6 [5: 6: 6: 7] sts.
Return to sts left on holder, rejoin appropriate yarn with RS facing and K to end.
Keeping stripes correct throughout, cont as folls:
Work 1 row.
Next row (RS): K2, sl 1, K1, psso, K to end.
Working all back neck decreases as set by last row, complete to match first side, reversing shapings.

FRONT

Work as given for back to **.
Cont in striped st st until 2 rows less have been worked than on back to beg of shoulder shaping, ending with RS facing for next row.
Shape front neck
Next row (RS): K21 [22: 23: 25: 26] and turn, leaving rem sts on a holder.
Work each side of neck separately.
Keeping stripes correct, dec 1 st at neck edge of next row. 20 [21: 22: 24: 25] sts.

Shape shoulder

Keeping stripes correct, dec 1 st at neck edge of next 4 rows, ending with RS facing for next row, **and at same time** cast off 5 [6: 6: 7: 7] sts at beg of next and foll alt row.

Cast off rem 6 [5: 6: 6: 7] sts.

Return to sts left on holder and slip centre 22 [26: 28: 30: 34] sts onto a holder (for neckband). Rejoin appropriate yarn with RS facing and K to end. Complete to match first side, reversing shapings.

MAKING UP

Press as described on the information page.
Join both shoulder seams.

Neckband

With RS facing, using 3¼mm (US 3) circular needle and yarn A, pick up and knit 5 sts down left side of front neck, K across 22 [26: 28: 30: 34] sts on front holder inc 1 st at centre, pick up and knit 5 sts up right side of front neck, and 52 [56: 60: 66: 68] sts down right side of back neck, 1 st from base of V neck and mark this st with a coloured thread, then pick up and knit 52 [56: 60: 66: 68] sts up left side of back neck. 138 [150: 160: 176: 182] sts. Join to work in rnds, placing marker for beg of rnd.

Round 1 (RS): *K1, P1, rep from * to within 3 sts of marked st, K1, K2tog, P marked st, sl 1, K1, psso, **K1, P1, rep from ** to end.
This row sets position of rib.
Keeping rib correct, cont as folls:
Round 2: Rib to within 2 sts of marked st, K2tog, P marked st, sl 1, K1, psso, rib to end.
Rep last round 5 times more. 124 [136: 146: 162: 168] sts.
Cast off in rib, still decreasing either side of marked st as before.
Mark points along side seam edges 14 [15: 16.5: 18: 20] cm either side of shoulder seams (to denote base of armhole openings).

Armhole borders (both alike)

With RS facing, using 3¼mm (US 3) needles and yarn A, pick up and knit 55 [59: 65: 71: 79] sts evenly along armhole opening edge between marked points.
Beg with row 2, work in rib as given for back for 7 rows, ending with RS facing for next row.
Cast off in rib.
See information page for finishing instructions.

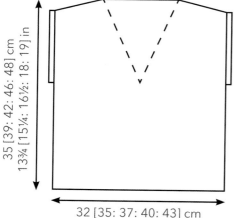

35 [39: 42: 46: 48] cm
13¾ [15¼: 16½: 18: 19] in

32 [35: 37: 40: 43] cm
12½ [13¾: 14½: 15¾: 17] in

Cub

quail studio

★ ☆ ☆ ☆

SIZE

To fit age						
	3-4	5-6	7-8	9-10	11-12	years
To fit chest						
	53-56	59-61	64-66	69-74	76-79	cm
	21-22	23-24	25-26	27-29	30-31	in
Actual chest measurement of garment						
	75	82	88	94	100	cm
	29½	32½	34½	37	39½	in

YARN

Rowan Brushed Fleece

4	4	4	5	5	x 50gm

(photographed in Cove 251 & Cairn 263)

NEEDLES

1 pair 5½mm (no 5) (US 9) needles
1 pair 6mm (no 4) (US 10) needles

EXTRAS

Stitch holders

TENSION

13 sts and 19 rows to 10 cm / 4 in measured over st st using 6mm (US 10) needles.

BACK

Using 5½mm (US 9) needles cast on 49 [53: 57: 61: 65] sts.
Row 1 (RS): K1 [0: 0: 2: 0], P2 [0: 2: 2: 1], *K3, P2, rep from * to last 1 [3: 0: 2: 4] sts, K1 [3: 0: 2: 3], P0 [0: 0: 0: 1].
Row 2: P1 [0: 0: 2: 0], K2 [0: 2: 2: 1], *P3, K2, rep from * to last 1 [3: 0: 2: 4] sts, P1 [3: 0: 2: 3], K0 [0: 0: 0: 1].
These 2 rows form rib.
Cont in rib until back meas 6 [7: 7: 8: 8] cm, ending with RS facing for next row.
Change to 6mm (US 10) needles.
Beg with a K row, now work in st st throughout as folls:
Cont straight until back meas 27.5 [31: 34: 36: 37.5] cm, ending with RS facing for next row.
Shape armholes
Cast off 2 sts at beg of next 2 rows. 45 [49: 53: 57: 61] sts.
Dec 1 st at each end of next and foll alt row. 41 [45: 49: 53: 57] sts.
Cont straight until armhole meas 15.5 [17: 18: 20: 21.5] cm, ending with RS facing for next row.

Shape shoulders and back neck
Next row (RS): Cast off 6 [7: 7: 8: 9] sts, K until there are 9 [10: 11: 11: 12] sts on right needle and turn, leaving rem sts on a holder.
Work each side of neck separately.
Cast off 3 sts at beg of next row.
Cast off rem 6 [7: 8: 8: 9] sts.
Return to sts left on holder and slip centre 11 [11: 13: 15: 15] sts onto another holder (for neckband). Rejoin yarn with RS facing and K to end. Complete to match first side, reversing shapings.

FRONT

Work as given for back until 6 [8: 8: 8: 10] rows less have been worked than on back to beg of shoulder shaping, ending with RS facing for next row.
Shape front neck
Next row (RS): K15 [18: 19: 20: 23] and turn, leaving rem sts on a holder.
Work each side of neck separately.
Dec 1 st at neck edge of next 2 rows, then on foll 1 [2: 2: 2: 3] alt rows. 12 [14: 15: 16: 18] sts.
Work 1 row, ending with RS facing for next row.
Shape shoulder
Cast off 6 [7: 7: 8: 9] sts at beg of next row.
Work 1 row.
Cast off rem 6 [7: 8: 8: 9] sts.
Return to sts left on holder and slip centre 11 [9: 11: 13: 11] sts onto another holder (for neckband). Rejoin yarn with RS facing and K to end. Complete to match first side, reversing shapings.

SLEEVES

Using 5½mm (US 9) needles cast on 25 [27: 27: 29: 29] sts.

Row 1 (RS): K0 [0: 0: 1: 1], P1 [2: 2: 2: 2], *K3, P2, rep from * to last 4 [0: 0: 1: 1] sts, K3 [0: 0: 1: 1], P1 [0: 0: 0: 0].

Row 2: P0 [0: 0: 1: 1], K1 [2: 2: 2: 2], *P3, K2, rep from * to last 4 [0: 0: 1: 1] sts, P3 [0: 0: 1: 1], K1 [0: 0: 0: 0].

These 2 rows form rib.

Cont in rib until sleeve meas 4 [5: 5: 6: 6] cm, ending with RS facing for next row.

Change to 6mm (US 10) needles.

Beg with a K row, now work in st st throughout as folls:

Work 2 rows, ending with RS facing for next row.

Next row (RS): K2, M1, K to last 2 sts, M1, K2. 27 [29: 29: 31: 31] sts.

Working all sleeve increases as set by last row, inc 1 st at each end of 4th and every foll 4th row to 31 [33: 37: 41: 43] sts, then on every foll 6th row until there are 37 [41: 45: 49: 53] sts.

Cont straight until sleeve meas 24 [28: 32: 36: 41] cm, ending with RS facing for next row.

Shape top

Cast off 2 sts at beg of next 2 rows. 33 [37: 41: 45: 49] sts.

Dec 1 st at each end of next 2 rows, ending with RS facing for next row.

Cast off rem 29 [33: 37: 41: 45] sts.

MAKING UP

Press as described on the information page.
Join right shoulder seam.

Neckband

With RS facing and using 5½mm (US 9) needles, pick up and knit 7 [8: 8: 9: 10] sts down left side of front neck, K across 11 [9: 11: 13: 11] sts on front holder, pick up and knit 7 [8: 8: 9: 10] sts up right side of front neck, and 3 sts down right side of back neck, K across 11 [11: 13: 15: 15] sts on back holder inc 0 [0: 1: 0: 0] st at centre, then pick up and knit 3 sts up left side of back neck. 42 [42: 47: 52: 52] sts.

Row 1 (WS): K2, *P3, K2, rep from * to end.
Row 2: P2, *K3, P2, rep from * to end.
These 2 rows form rib.

Cont in rib until neckband meas 6 [7: 7: 8: 8] cm, ending with RS facing for next row.

Cast off **very loosely** in rib, taking care cast-off edge will stretch over child's head.

Join left shoulder and neckband seam. See information page for finishing instructions, setting in sleeves using the shallow set-in method.

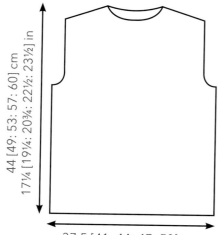

44 [49: 53: 57: 60] cm
17¼ [19¼: 20¾: 22½: 23½] in

37.5 [41: 44: 47: 50] cm
14¾ [16¼: 17¼: 18½: 19¾] in

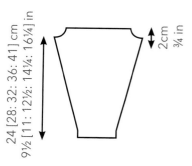

24 [28: 32: 36: 41] cm
9½ [11: 12½: 14¼: 16¼] in

2 cm
¾ in

Haze
quail studio
★ ★ ★ ☆

SIZE

To fit age						
	3-4	5-6	7-8	9-10	11-12	years
To fit chest						
	53-56	59-61	64-66	69-74	76-79	cm
	21-22	23-24	25-26	27-29	30-31	in
Actual chest measurement of garment						
	68	75	78	85	92	cm
	27	29½	31	33½	36	in

YARN

Rowan Big Wool

8	9	10	10	11	x 100gm

(photographed in Prize 64)

NEEDLES
1 pair 8mm (no 0) (US 11) needles
8mm (no 0) (US 11) circular needle at least 80 [90: 100: 110: 120] cm long

EXTRAS
Stitch holder
Stitch markers

TENSION
12 sts and 26 rows to 10 cm / 4 in measured over g st using 8mm (US 11) needles.

SPECIAL ABBREVIATION
MB = make bobble as folls: K into front, back, front and back again of next st, slip these 4 sts back onto left needle, K4, slip these 4 sts back onto left needle, K4, lift 4th, 3rd and 2nd sts on right needle over first st and off right needle.

BACK
Using 8mm (US 11) needles cast on 41 [47: 47: 53: 56] sts.
Row 1 (RS): P2, *K1, P2, rep from * to end.
Row 2: K2, *P1, K2, rep from * to end.
These 2 rows form rib.
Cont in rib for a further 4 [4: 6: 6: 6] rows, dec - [2: -: 2: 1] sts evenly across last row and ending with RS facing for next row. 41 [45: 47: 51: 55] sts.
Beg with a RS row, now work in g st throughout as folls:
Cont straight until back meas 53 [58: 63: 68: 72] cm, ending with RS facing for next row.

Shape shoulders
Cast off 6 [6: 6: 7: 7] sts at beg of next 2 rows, then 6 [7: 7: 7: 8] sts at beg of foll 2 rows.
Break yarn and leave rem 17 [19: 21: 23: 25] sts on a holder.

LEFT FRONT
Using 8mm (US 11) needles cast on 14 [14: 14: 14: 17] sts.
Work in rib as given for back for 6 [6: 8: 8: 8] rows, dec 2 [1: 1: -: 2] sts evenly across last row and ending with RS facing for next row. 12 [13: 13: 14: 15] sts.
Beg with a RS row, now work in g st throughout as folls:
Cont straight until left front matches back to beg of shoulder shaping, ending with RS facing for next row.

Shape shoulders
Cast off 6 [6: 6: 7: 7] sts at beg of next row.
Work 1 row.
Cast off rem 6 [7: 7: 7: 8] sts.

RIGHT FRONT
Work as given for left front, reversing shapings.

SLEEVES
Using 8mm (US 11) needles cast on 23 [23: 23: 26: 26] sts.
Work in rib as given for back for 6 [6: 8: 8: 8] rows, inc 0 [2: 2: 1: 1] sts evenly across last row and ending with RS facing for next row. 23 [25: 25: 27: 27] sts.
Now work in bobble patt as folls:
Row 1 (RS): K3 [4: 4: 1: 1], MB, *K3, MB, rep from * to last 3 [4: 4: 1: 1] sts, K3 [4: 4: 1: 1].
Row 2: Purl.
Row 3: K1 [2: 2: 3: 3], MB, *K3, MB, rep from * to last 1 [2: 2: 3: 3] sts, K1 [2: 2: 3: 3].
Row 4: Purl.

These 4 rows form bobble patt.

Work in bobble patt for a further 6 rows, inc 1 st at each end of 3rd of these rows (taking inc sts into patt) and ending with RS facing for next row. 25 [27: 27: 29: 29] sts.

Now work in g st throughout as folls:

Inc 1 st at each end of 5th and every foll 8th row until there are 33 [35: 37: 39: 47] sts, then on - [1: 1: 2: -] foll 10th rows. - [37: 39: 43: -] sts.

Cont straight until sleeve meas 23 [27: 31: 37: 40] cm, ending with RS facing for next row. Cast off.

MAKING UP

Press as described on the information page.

Join both shoulder seams.

Front band

With RS facing and using 8mm (US 11) circular needle, beg and ending at front cast-on edges, pick up and knit 65 [70: 77: 83: 88] sts up right front opening edge to shoulder, K across 17 [19: 21: 23: 25] sts on back holder inc 1 [1: 0: 1: 1] st at centre, then pick up and knit 65 [70: 77: 83: 88] sts down left front opening edge. 148 [160: 175: 190: 202] sts.

Row 1 (WS): Knit.

Row 2: Knit.

Row 3: K1, *P2, K1, rep from * to end.

Row 4: P1, *K2, P1, rep from * to end.

Last 2 rows form rib.

Cont in rib until band meas 6 [6: 7: 7: 7] cm from pick-up row, ending with RS facing for next row. Cast off in rib.

Mark points along side seam edges 14 [16: 17: 18: 20] cm either side of shoulder seams (to denote base of armhole openings). See information page for finishing instructions, setting in sleeves using the straight cast-off method.

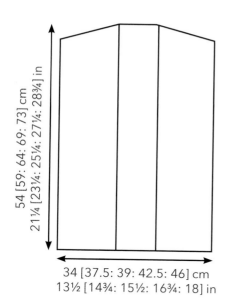

54 [59: 64: 69: 73] cm
21¼ [23¼: 25¼: 27¼: 28¾] in

34 [37.5: 39: 42.5: 46] cm
13½ [14¾: 15½: 16¾: 18] in

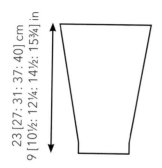

23 [27: 31: 37: 40] cm
9 [10½: 12¼: 14½: 15¾] in

SIZE
To fit age

3-7	9-12	years

Width around head (unstretched)

41	46	cm
16¼	18	in

YARN
Rowan Big Wool

1	1	x 100gm

(photographed in Prize 64 & Ice Blue 21)

NEEDLES
1 pair 7mm (no 2) (US 10½) needles

EXTRAS – Rowan faux fur pom pom

TENSION
12 sts and 24 rows to 10 cm / 4 in measured over g st using 7mm (US 10½) needles.

HAT
Using 7mm (US 10½) needles cast on 49 [55] sts.
Row 1 (RS): K1, *P1, K1, rep from * to end.
Row 2: P1, *K1, P1, rep from * to end.
These 2 rows form rib.
Cont in rib for a further 6 [8] rows, ending with RS facing for next row.
Now work in g st throughout as folls:
Cont straight until hat meas 15 [16] cm, ending with RS facing for next row.
Shape top
Row 1 (RS): (K4, K2tog) 8 [9] times, K1. 41 [46] sts.
Work 3 rows.
Row 5: (K3, K2tog) 8 [9] times, K1. 33 [37] sts.
Work 1 row.
Row 7: (K2, K2tog) 8 [9] times, K1. 25 [28] sts.
Work 1 row.
Row 9: (K1, K2tog) 8 [9] times, K1. 17 [19] sts.
Work 1 row.
Row 11: (K2tog) 8 [9] times, K1. 9 [10] sts.
Work 1 row, ending with RS facing for next row.
Break yarn and thread through rem 9 [10] sts. Pull up tight and fasten off securely.

MAKING UP
Press as described on the information page. Join back seam. If desired, attach pompom to top of hat. See information page for finishing instructions.

Information

TENSION

Obtaining the correct tension is perhaps the single factor which can make the difference between a successful garment and a disastrous one. It controls both the shape and size of an article, so any variation, however slight, can distort the finished garment. Different designers feature in our books and it is their tension, given at the start of each pattern, which you must match. We recommend that you knit a square in pattern and/ or stocking stitch (depending on the pattern instructions) of perhaps 5 - 10 more stitches and 5 - 10 more rows than those given in the tension note. Mark out the central 10cm square with pins. If you have too many stitches to 10cm try again using thicker needles, if you have too few stitches to 10cm try again using finer needles. Once you have achieved the correct tension your garment will be knitted to the measurements indicated in the size diagram shown at the end of the pattern.

CHART NOTE

Many of the patterns in the book are worked from charts. Each square on a chart represents a stitch and each line of squares a row of knitting. Each colour used is given a different letter and these are shown in the materials section, or in the key alongside the chart of each pattern. When working from the charts, read odd rows (K) from right to left and even rows (P) from left to right, unless otherwise stated. When working lace from a chart it is important to note that all but the largest size may have to alter the first and last few stitches in order not to lose or gain stitches over the row.

WORKING A LACE PATTERN

When working a lace pattern it is important to remember that if you are unable to work both the increase and corresponding decrease and vica versa, the stitches should be worked in stocking stitch.

KNITTING WITH COLOUR

There are two main methods of working colour into a knitted fabric: Intarsia and Fairisle techniques. The first method produces a single thickness of fabric and is usually used where a colour is only required in a particular area of a row and does not form a repeating pattern across the row, as in the fairisle technique.

Fairisle type knitting: When two or three colours are worked repeatedly across a row, strand the yarn not in use loosely behind the stitches being worked. If you are working with more than two colours, treat the "floating" yarns as if they were one yarn and always spread the stitches to their correct width to keep them elastic. It is advisable not to carry the stranded or "floating" yarns over more than three stitches at a time, but to weave them under and over the colour you are working. The "floating" yarns are therefore caught at the back of the work.

Intarsia: The simplest way to do this is to cut short lengths of yarn for each motif or block of colour used in a row.Then joining in the various colours at the appropriate point on the row, link one colour to the next by twisting them around each other where they meet on the wrong side to avoid gaps. All ends can then either be darned along the colour join lines, as each motif is completed or then can be "knitted-in" to the fabric of the knitting as each colour is worked into the pattern. This is done in much the same way as "weaving- in" yarns when working the Fairisle technique and does save time darning-in ends. It is essential that the tension is noted for intarsia as this may vary from the stocking stitch if both are used in the same pattern.

After working for hours knitting a garment, it seems a great pity that many garments are spoiled because such little care is taken in the pressing and finishing process. Follow the text below for a truly professional-looking garment.

Block out each piece of knitting and following the instructions on the ball band press the garment pieces, omitting the ribs. Tip: Take special care to press the edges, as this will make sewing up both easier and neater. If the ball band indicates that the fabric is not to be pressed, then covering the blocked out fabric with a damp white cotton cloth and leaving it to stand will have the desired effect. Darn in all ends neatly along the selvage edge or a colour join, as appropriate.

STITCHING

When stitching the pieces together, remember to match areas of colour and texture very carefully where they meet. Use a seam stitch such as back stitch or mattress stitch for all main knitting seams and join all ribs and neckband with mattress stitch, unless otherwise stated.

CONSTRUCTION

Having completed the pattern instructions, join left shoulder and neckband seams as detailed above. Sew the top of the sleeve to the body of the garment using the method detailed in the pattern, referring to the appropriate guide:

Straight cast-off sleeves: Place centre of cast-off edge of sleeve to shoulder seam. Sew top of sleeve to body, using markers as guidelines where applicable.

Square set-in sleeves: Place centre of cast-off edge of sleeve to shoulder seam. Set sleeve head into armhole, the straight sides at top of sleeve to form a neat right-angle to cast-off sts at armhole on back and front.

Shallow set-in sleeves: Place centre of cast off edge of sleeve to shoulder seam. Match decreases at beg of armhole shaping to decreases at top of sleeve. Sew sleeve head into armhole, easing in shapings.

Set-in sleeves: Place centre of cast-off edge of sleeve to shoulder seam. Set in sleeve, easing sleeve head into armhole. Join side and sleeve seams.
Slip stitch pocket edgings and linings into place. Sew on buttons to correspond with buttonholes. Ribbed welts and neckbands and any areas of garter stitch should not be pressed.

ABBREVIATIONS

K	knit
P	purl
st(s)	stitch(es)
inc	increas(e)(ing)
dec	decreas(e)(ing)
st st	stocking stitch (1 row K, 1 row P)
g st	garter stitch (K every row)
beg	begin(ning)
foll	following
rem	remain(ing)
rev st st	reverse stocking stitch (1 row K , 1 row P)
rep	repeat
rnd	round
alt	alternate
cont	continue
patt	pattern
tog	together
mm	millimetres
cm	centimetres
in(s)	inch(es)
RS	right side
WS	wrong side
sl 1	slip one stitch
psso	pass slipped stitch over
p2sso	pass 2 slipped stitches over
tbl	through back of loop
M1	make one stitch by picking up horizontal loop before next stitch and knitting into back of it
M1P	make one stitch by picking up horizontal loop before next stitch and purlinginto back of it
yfwd	yarn forward
yrn	yarn round needle
meas	measures
0	no stitches, times or rows
-	no stitches, times or rows for that size
yo	yarn over needle
yfrn	yarn forward round needle
wyib	with yarn at back
sl2togK	slip 2 stitches together knitways

BUTTONS & RIBBON

Groves & Banks
Eastern Bypass
Thame
Oxfordshire
OX9 3FU
www.grovesltd.co.uk
groves@stockistenquiries.co.uk

Bedecked Haberdashery
The Coach House
Barningham Park
RICHMOND
DL11 7DW
Tel: +44 (0)1833 621 451
eMail:Judith.lewis@bedecked.co.uk
www.bedecked.co.uk

EXPERIENCE RATING
for guidance only

★ Beginner Techniques

For the beginner knitter, basic garment shaping and straight forward stitch technique.

★ ★ Simple Techniques

Simple straight forward knitting, introducing various, shaping techniques and garments.

★ ★ ★ Experienced Techniques

For the more experienced knitter, using more advanced shaping techniques at the same time as colourwork or more advanced stitch techniques.

★ ★ ★ ★ Advanced Techniques

Advanced techniques used, using advanced stitches and garment shaping along with more challenging techniques.

MODEL SIZE INFORMATION
Tiegan wears 5-6 years
Janae wears 9-10 years

WASH CARE INFORMATION

You may have noticed over the last season that the wash care symbols on our ball bands and shade cards have changed. This is to bring the symbols we use up to date and hopefully help you to care for your knitting and crochet more easily. Below are the symbols you are likely to see and a brief explanation of each.

MACHINE WASH SYMBOLS

HAND WASH SYMBOLS

DRY CLEAN SYMBOLS

IRONING SYMBOLS

DO NOT BLEACH SYMBOL

DRYING SYMBOLS

Sizing Guide

When you knit a children's design, we want you to be happy with the look and feel of the finished garment. This all starts with the size and fit of the design you choose. To help you to achieve the correct fit for your child, please refer to the sizing chart below.

Dimensions in the chart are body measurements, not garment dimensions, therefore please refer to the measuring guide to help you to determine which is the best size for your child.

STANDARD SIZING GUIDE FOR CHILDREN

AGE	3 - 4 yrs	5 - 6 yrs	7 - 8 yrs	9 - 10 yrs	11 - 12 yrs	
To fit height	98 - 104	110 - 116	122 - 128	134 - 140	146 - 152	cm
To fit chest	31	34	36	39	42	cm
	12.¼	13½	14¼	15¼	16½	in
To fit waist	30	32	34	36	38	cm
	11¾	13½	13½	14¼	15	in

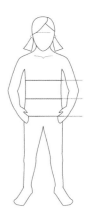

SIZING & SIZE DIAGRAM NOTE

The instructions are given for the smallest size. Where they vary, work the figures in brackets for the larger sizes. One set of figures refers to all sizes. Included with most patterns in this magazine is a 'size diagram' - see image on the right, of the finished garment and its dimensions. The measurement shown at the bottom of each 'size diagram' shows the garment width 2.5cm below the armhole shaping. To help you choose the size of garment to knit please refer to the sizing guide. Generally in the majority of designs the welt width (at the cast on edge of the garment) is the same width as the chest. However, some designs are 'A-Line' in shape or flared edge and in these cases welt width will be wider than the chest width.

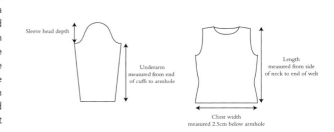

MEASURING GUIDE

For maximum comfort and to ensure the correct fit when choosing the size to knit, please follow the tips below when checking the size of your baby or child.
Measure as close to the body over underwear, but don't pull the tape measure too tight!

Height
measure from the top of your child's head to their feet when they are laying or standing straight.
Chest
measure around the fullest part of the chest and across the shoulder blades.
Waist
measure around the natural waistline just above the hip bone.
Hips
measure around the fullest part of the bottom.

If you don't wish to measure your child's, note the size of their or your favourite jumper that you like the fit of. Our sizes are comparable to the clothing sizes from the major high street retailers, so if the favourite jumper is 6 months or 3 years, then our 6 months or 3 years size should measure approximately the same. Measure this favourite jumper and compare the measurements against the size diagram at the end of the pattern you wish to knit.

Finally, once you have decided which size is best for you to knit, please ensure that you achieve the correct tension for the design you are planning to knit.

Remember if your tension is too loose, your garment will be bigger than the pattern size and you may use more yarn. If your tension is too tight, your garment will be smaller than the pattern size and you may have yarn left over. Furthermore if your tension is incorrect, the handle of your fabric will be either too stiff or too floppy and will not fit properly. As you invest money and time in knitting one of our designs, it really does make sense to check your tension before starting your project.

Anleitungen

GRÖSSEN

Alter						
	3-4	5-6	7-8	9-10	11-12	Jahre
Passend für Brustumfang						
	53-56	59-61	64-66	69-74	76-79	cm
Gestrickter Brustumfang						
	69	74	79	86	93	cm

GARN
Rowan Alpaca Classic
Tunika mit rundem Halsausschnitt

	5	5	6	7	8	x 25g

(fotografiert in Soft Satin 116)
Tunika mit V-Ausschnitt

	5	5	6	7	8	x 25g

(fotografiert in Snowflake White 115)

NADELN
Stricknadeln 3 ¼ mm und 3 ¾ mm
1 Rundstrickndl 3 ¼ mm, höchstens 30 cm lang
(oder ein Nadelspiel mit 4 Nadeln)

EXTRAS
Hilfsnadeln
Maschenmarkierer (Mm)

MASCHENPROBE
23 M und 31 R = 10 x 10 cm, glatt re gestr mit Ndl
Nr. 3 ¾ mm.

Tunika mit rundem Halsausschnitt

RÜCKENTEIL
79 (85: 91: 99: 107) M mit Ndl Nr. 3 ¼ mm anschl.
R 1 (RS): 1 M re, *1 M li, 1 M re, ab * wdhl bis zum
Ende.
R 2: 1 M li, *1 M re, 1 M li, ab * wdhl bis zum Ende.
Die 2 R bilden das Rippenmuster, weitere 6 (6: 8:
8: 8) R str, enden mit einer Rückr.
Wechseln zur Ndl Nr. 3 ¾ mm.
Mit einer Rechtsr beg und fortlfd glatt re str bis
35 (39: 43: 45,5: 48,5) cm erreicht sind, enden mit
einer Rückr.
Armausschnitte
Am Anf der nächsten 2 R je 3 (3: 4: 4: 5) M abk =
73 (79: 83: 91: 97) M.
An den Armausschnitten in den nächsten 3 (3: 3:
5: 5) R bds je 1 M abn, danach 3 (4: 4: 4: 4) x in
jeder folg 2. R = 61 (65: 69: 73: 79) M.

Nach einer Armausschnittlänge von 12,5 (13,5:
14,5: 16: 17) cm enden mit einer Rückr.
Schulterschrägen und rückw Halsausschnitt
Nächste R (Hinr): 5 (5: 6: 6: 7) M abk, re str bis
13 (14: 14: 15: 16) M auf der re Ndl sind, Arb
wenden, die restl M auf einer Hilfsndl stilllegen,
beide Seiten getrennt beenden.
Am Halsausschnitt in den nächsten 3 R je 1 M
abn, enden mit einer Rückr, **gleichzeitig** am
Halsausschnitt in den nächsten 3 R je 1 M abn,
enden mit einer Rückr, **gleichzeitig** am Anf der 2. R
5 (5: 6: 6: 7) M abk.
Die restl 5 (6: 5: 6: 6) M abk.
Die stillgelegten M aufn, die mittl 25 (27: 29:
31: 33) M auf einer Hilfsndl stilllegen, mit neuem
Fd in einer Hinr re str bis zum Ende.
Die 2. Seite gegengleich beenden.

VORDERTEIL
Genauso str wie das Rückenteil bis 10 (12: 12:
12: 14) R unterhalb des Beg der Schulterschrägen,
enden mit einer Rückr.
Vord Halsausschnitt
Nächste R (Hinr): 22 (24: 25: 26: 29) M re, Arb
wenden, die restl M auf einer Hilfsndl stilllegen,
beide Seiten getrennt beenden.
Am Halsausschnitt in den nächsten 4 R je 1 M abn,

danach 2 (3: 3: 3: 4) x in jeder folg 2. R = 16 (17: 18: 19: 21) M.
1 R str, enden mit einer Rückr.

Schulterschräge
Am Anf der nächsten R und am Anf der folg 2. R je 5 (5: 6: 6: 7) M abk, **gleichzeitig** am Halsausschnitt in der nächsten R 1 M abn.
1 R str.
Die restl 5 (6: 5: 6: 6) M abk.
Die stillgelegten M aufn, die mittl 17 (17: 19: 21: 21) M auf einer Hilfsndl stilllegen, mit neuem Fd in einer Hinr re str bis zum Ende.
Die 2. Seite gegengleich beenden.

ÄRMEL
35 (37: 37: 39: 41) M mit Ndl Nr. 3 ¼ mm anschl.
8 (8: 10: 10: 10) R im Ripp str so wie beim Rückenteil angegeben, enden mit einer Rückr.
Wechseln zur Ndl Nr. 3 ¾ mm.
Mit einer Rechtsr beg und fortlfd glatt re str, dabei für die seitl Zun in der 5. (7.: 5.: 5.: 5.) R und 2 (0: 4: 5: 2) x in jeder folg 6. R bds je 1 M zun, danach in jeder folg 8. R bis 49 (53: 57: 63: 67) M erreicht sind.
Nach einer Länge von 23 (27: 31: 35: 40) cm enden mit einer Rückr.

Armkugel
Am Anf der nächsten 2 R je 3 (3: 4: 4: 5) M abk = 43 (47: 49: 55: 57) M.
In der nächsten R und 1 x in der folg 2. R bds je 1 M abn, danach 2 x in jeder folg 4. R = 35 (39: 41: 47: 49) M.
1 R str.
In der nächsten R und 2 (3: 5: 5: 7) x in jeder folg 2. R bds je 1 M abn, danach in den nächsten 7 (7: 5: 7: 5) R, enden mit einer Rückr.
Die restl 15 (17: 19: 21: 23) M abk.

FERTIGSTELLUNG
Alle Teile dämpfen, siehe Informationsseite.
Beide Schulternähte schließen.

Halsblende
Von re mit der Rundstrickndl Nr. 3 ¼ mm die M wie folgt aufn und re str: Aus der li vord Halsausschnittkante 13 (15: 15: 15: 17) M, die 17 (17: 19: 21: 21) M auf der Hilfsndl im Vorderteil re str, aus der re vord Halsausschnittkante 13 (15: 15: 15: 17) M, aus der re rückw Halsausschnittkante 3 M, die 25 (27: 29: 31: 33) M auf der Hilfsndl im Rückenteil re str und aus der li rückw Halsausschnittkante 3 M = 74 (80: 84: 88: 94) M.
In Runden str wie folgt, dabei Anf und Ende jeder Rde markieren:
Rde 1 (RS): *1 M re, 1 M li, ab * wdhl bis zum Ende.
Weitere 4 Runden im Rippenmuster str, danach alle M so locker abk, dass der Pullover über den Kopf passt.

Die Ärmel in die Armausschnitte nähen, die Seiten- und Ärmelnähte schließen.

Tunika mit V-Ausschnitt

RÜCKENTEIL
Genauso str wie bei der Tunika mit rundem Halsausschnitt angegeben.

VORDERTEIL
Genauso str wie die Tunika mit rundem Halsausscshnitt bis 22 (24: 24: 24: 26) R unterhalb des Beg der Schulterschrägen, enden mit einer Rückr.

Vord Halsausschnitt
Nächste R (Hinr): 30 (32: 34: 36: 39) M re, Arb wenden, die restl M auf einer Hilfsndl stilllegen, beide Seiten getrennt beenden.
Am Halsausschnitt in den nächsten 12 (12: 14: 14: 16) R je 1 M abn, danach 3 (4: 3: 4: 3) x in jeder folg 2. R = 15 (16: 17: 18: 20) M.
3 R str, enden mit einer Rückr.

Schulterschräge
Am Anf der nächsten R und am Anf der folg 2. R je 5 (5: 6: 6: 7) M abk.
1 R str, danach die restl 5 (6: 5: 6: 6) M abk.
Die stillgelegten M aufn, die mittl M auf einer Hilfsndl stilllegen, mit neuem Fd in einer Hinr re str bis zum Ende = 30 (32: 34: 36: 39) M.
Die 2. Seite gegengleich beenden.

ÄRMEL
Genauso str wie bei der Tunika mit rundem Halsausschnitt angegeben.

FERTIGSTELLUNG
Alle Teile dämpfen, siehe Informationsseite.
Beide Schulternähte schließen.

Halsblende
Von re mit der Rundstrickndl Nr. 3 ¼ mm die M wie folgt aufn und re str: Aus der li vord Halsausschnittkante 22 (24: 24: 24: 26) M, die M auf der Hilfsndl in der vord Mitte re str und mit einem Kontrastfaden markieren, aus der re vord Halsausschnittkante 22 (24: 24: 24: 26) M, aus der re rückw Halsausschnittkante 3 M, die 25 (27: 29: 31: 33) M auf der Hilfsndl im Rückenteil re str und aus der li rückw Halsausschnittkante 3 M = 76 (82: 84: 86: 92) M. In Runden str wie folgt, dabei Anf und Ende jeder Rde markieren:
Rde 1 (Hinr): *1 M re, 1 M li, ab * wdhl bis zum Ende.
Diese Rde teilt das Rippenmuster ein.
Rde 2: Im Ripp str bis 1 M vor der mark M, die nächsten 2 M wie zum 2 M re zus-str abheben (die 2. M ist die abgehobene M), 1 M re, danach die 2 abgehobenen M überziehen, im Ripp bis zum Ende.

Die letzte Rde noch 3 xwdhl = 68 (74: 76: 78: 84) M.
Alle M **sehr locker** abk, dabei die Abn bds der
mittl M noch 1 x wdhl. Der Pullover muss über den
Kopf des Kindes passen.
Die Ärmel in die Armausschnitte nähen, die Seiten-
und Ärmelnähte schließen.

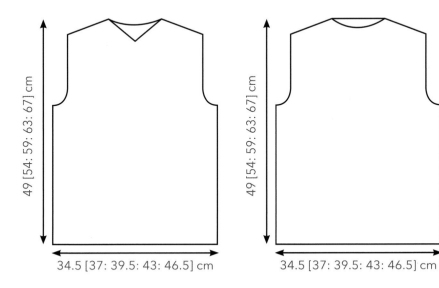

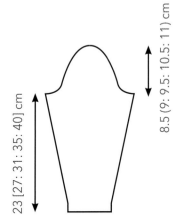

Dream
quail studio
★ ★ ☆ ☆

GRÖSSEN

Alter						
	3-4	5-6	7-8	9-10	11-12	Jahre
Brustumfang						
	53-56	59-61	64-66	69-74	76-79	cm
Gestrickter Brustumfang						
	73	78	83	93	98	cm

GARN
Rowan Big Wool

5	5	6	6	7	x 100g

(fotografiert in Ice Blue 21)

NADELN
Stricknadeln 10 mm
Zopfndl

EXTRAS
Hilfsnadeln
Maschenmarkierer (Mm)

MASCHENPROBE
8 M und 16 R = 10 x 10 cm, kraus re gestr mit Ndl Nr. 10 mm.

RÜCKENTEIL
29 (31: 33: 37: 39) M mit Ndl Nr. 10 mm anschl.
R 1 (Hinr): 1 M re, *1 M li, 1 M re, ab * wdhl bis zum Ende.
R 2: 1 M li, *1 M re, 1 M li, ab * wdhl bis zum Ende.
Diese 2 R bilden das Rippenmuster und werden wdhl bis 4 (4: 5: 5: 5) cm erreicht sind, enden mit einer Rückr.
Weiter kraus re str bis 40 (44: 48: 52: 55) cm erreicht sind, enden mit einer Rückr.
Schultern
Am Anf der nächsten 2 R je 8 (9: 9: 11: 11) M abk.
Den Fd abschneiden, die restl 13 (13: 15: 15: 17) M auf einer Hilfsndl stilllegen (für die Halsblende).

VORDERTEIL
Genauso str wie das Rückenteil bis 8 (8: 8: 8: 10) R unterhalb der Schultern, enden mit einer Rückr.
Vord Halsausschnitt
Nächste R (Hinr): 12 (13: 13: 15: 16) M re, Arb wenden, die restl M auf einer Hilfsndl stilllegen, beide Seiten getrennt beenden.
Am Halsausschnitt in den nächsten 2 R je 1 M abn, danach 2 (2: 2: 2: 3) x in jeder folg 2. R = 8 (9: 9: 11: 11) M.
1 R str, enden mit einer Rückr.

Schulter
Die restl 8 (9: 9: 11: 11) M abk.
Die stillgelegten M aufn, die mittl 5 (5: 7: 7: 7) M auf einer Hilfsndl stilllegen, mit neuem Fd in einer Hinr re str bis zum Ende.
Die 2. Seite gegengleich beenden.

ÄRMEL
15 (15: 15: 17: 17) M mit Ndl Nr. 10 mm anschl.
4 (4: 5: 5: 5) cm im Rippenmuster str so wie beim Rückenteil angegeben, enden mit einer Hinr.
Nächste R (Rückr): 5 (5: 5: 6: 6) M im Ripp, 2 x (in der nächsten M 1 M zun, 1 M im Ripp), in der nächsten M 1 M zun, 5 (5: 5: 6: 6) M im Ripp = 18 (18: 18: 20: 20) M.
Im Mst str wie folgt:
R 1 (Hinr): 5 (5: 5: 6: 6) M re, die nächsten 4 M auf eine ZN heben und nach hinten legen, 4 M re, danach die 4 M auf der ZN re str, 5 (5: 5: 6: 6) M re.
R 2: 5 (5: 5: 6: 6) M re, 8 M li, 5 (5: 5: 6: 6) M re.
R 3: Rechts.
R 4 und 5: Wie R 2 und 3.
R 6: Wie R 2.
Diese 6 R bilden das Mst und werden fortlfd wdhl, dabei für die seitl Zun in der 7. (3.: nächsten: 3.: 3.) R und in jeder folg 14. (12.: 10.: 10.: 10.) R bds je 1 M zun bis 22 (24: 26: 24: 28) M erreicht sind, danach in jeder folg – (–: –: 12.: 12.) R bis – (–: –: 28: 30) M erreicht sind, alle Zun kraus re str.
Nach einer Länge von 25 (29: 33: 37: 42) cm enden mit einer Rückr.
Alle M abk.

FERTIGSTELLUNG

Alle Teile dämpfen, siehe Informationsseite.
Die re Schulternaht schließen.

Halsblende

Von re mit Ndl Nr. 10 mm die M wie folgt aufn
und re str: Aus der li vord Halausschnittkante
7 (7: 7: 9: 9) M, die 5 (5: 7: 7: 7) M auf der
Hilfsndl im Vorderteil re str, aus der re vord
Halsausschnittkante 7 (7: 7: 9: 9) M, zuletzt die
13 (13: 15: 15: 17) M auf der Hilfsndl im Rückenteil
re str, dabei in der Mitte 1 M zun = 33 (33: 37:
41: 43) M.
Mit R 2 des Rippenmusters beg so wie beim
Rückenteil angegeben, nach 4 (4: 5: 5: 5) cm die
M **sehr locker** abk, der Ausschnitt muss über den
Kopf passen.
Die li Schulternaht und die seitl Blendennaht
schließen.
An allen seitl Rändern von den Schulternähten
abwärts je 13 (14: 15: 16,5: 18) cm abmessen
und markieren. Die Ärmel mit der Mitte der
Abkettkante auf die Schulternähte heften und an
den seitl Rändern zwischen den Markierungen
festnähen. Die Seiten- und Ärmelnähte schließen.

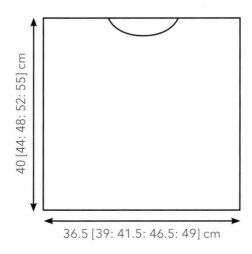

40 [44: 48: 52: 55] cm

36.5 [39: 41.5: 46.5: 49] cm

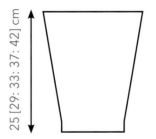

25 [29: 33: 37: 42] cm

GRÖSSE
Alter

	3-7	9-12	Jahre
Kopfumfang (nicht gedehnt)			
	37	41	cm

GARN
Rowan Alpaca Soft DK

	2	2	x 50g

(fotografiert in Rainy Day 210 & Simply White 201)

NADELN
Stricknadeln 6 mm

EXTRAS – 1 gekaufter Bommel (optional)

MASCHENPROBE
20 M und 22 R = 10 x 10 cm, im Ripp gestr mit Ndl Nr. 6 mm und doppeltem Fd.

MÜTZE
74 (82) M mit Ndl Nr. 6 und doppeltem Fd anschl.
R 1 (Hinr): 2 M re, *2 M li, 2 M re, ab * wdhl bis zum Ende.
R 2: 2 M li, *2 M re, 2 M li, ab * wdhl bis zum Ende.
Diese 2 R bilden das Rippenmuster und werden wdhl bis 17 (18) cm erreicht sind, enden mit einer Rückr.
Spitze
R 1 (Hinr): 2 M re, 9 (10) x (2 M li, 2 M re, 2 M li zus-str, 2 M re) = 65 (72) M.
R 2: 9 (10) x (2 M li, 1 M re, 2 M li, 2 M re), 2 M li.
R 3: 2 M re, 9 (10) x (2 M li, 2 M re, 1 M li, 2 M re).
R 4: Wie R 2.
R 5: 2 M re, 9 (10) x (2 M li zus-str, 2 M re, 1 M li, 2 M re) = 56 (62) M.
R 6: 18 (20) x (2 M li, 1 M re), 2 M li.
R 7: 2 M re, 18 (20) x (1 M li, 2 M re).
R 8: Wie R 6.
R 9: 2 M re, 9 (10) x (1 M li, 2 M re zus-str, 1 M li, 2 M re) = 47 (52) M.
R 10: 9 (10) x (2 M li, 1 M re, 1 M li, 1 M re), 2 M li.
R 11: 2 M re zus-str, 9 (10) x (1 M li, 1 M re, 1 M li, 2 M re zus-str) = 37 (41) M.
R 12: 1 M li, *1 M re, 1 M li, ab * wdhl bis zum Ende.
R 13: 1 M re, 9 (10) x (1 M li, übzAbn, 1 M re) = 28 (31) M.
R 14: 9 (10) x (2 M li, 1 M re), 1 M li.

R 15: 9 (10) x (übzAbn, 1 M re), 1 M re. 19 (21) M.
R 16: 9 (10) x (2 M li zus-str), 1 M li.
Den Fd abschneiden und durch die restl 10 (11) M ziehen, die M fest zusammenziehen, den Fd gut vernähen.

FERTIGSTELLUNG
Die Mütze dämpfen, siehe Informationsseite.
Die rückw Naht schließen, dabei die unteren 3 cm von der Gegenseite zunähen, weil der Rand nach außen umgeschlagen wird.
Falls gewünscht, einen Bommel auf der Mütze festnähen.

Tallulah
georgia farrell
★ ★ ★ ☆

GRÖSSE
Alter

	3-7	9-12	Jahre

GARN
Rowan Alpaca Soft DK

	4	5	x 50g

(fotografiert in Rainy Day 210)

NADELN
Je 1 Nadelspiel mit 4 Nadeln 3 ¾ mm und 4 mm.

EXTRAS
2 gekaufte Bommeln
Maschenmarkierer

MASCHENPROBE
19 M und 48 Runden = 10 x 10 cm, im Mst gestr mit Ndl Nr. 4 mm.

FERTIGE GRÖSSE
Der Schal ist 12 (15) cm breit und 115 (125) cm lang, ohne Bommeln.

SPEZIELLE ABKÜRZUNGEN
1 M re tiefer = Die M unterhalb der nächsten M auf der li Ndl re str, diese M mit der darüberliegenden M zus von der li Ndl fallen lassen; **1 M li tiefer** = Die M unterhalb der nächsten M auf der li Ndl li str, diese M mit der darüberliegenden M zus von der li Ndl fallen lassen.

SCHAL
46 (58) M mit dem Nadelspiel Nr. 3 ¾ mm anschl. Die M auf 3 der 4 Nadeln gleichmäßig verteilen, in Runden str wie folgt, dabei beachten, dass in der 1. Rde die M nicht verdreht sind, Anf und Ende jeder Rde markieren:
Rde 1 (Hinr): *1 M re, 1 M li, ab * wdhl bis zum Ende. Diese Rde teilt das Rippenmuster ein und wird wdhl bis 3 (4) cm erreicht sind.
Wechseln zum Nadelspiel Nr. 4 mm.
Im Mst str wie folgt:

Rde 1: *1 M re, 1 M li tiefer, ab * wdhl bis zum Ende.
Rde 2: *1 M re tiefer, 1 M li, ab * wdhl bis zum Ende.
Die beiden Runden bilden das Mst und werden wdhl bis 112 (121) cm erreicht sind.
Wechseln zum Nadelspiel Nr. 3 ¾ mm.
Im Ripp str bis 3 (4) cm erreicht sind, danach alle M im Ripp abk.

FERTIGSTELLUNG
Den Schal dämpfen, siehe Informationsseite. Durch die Abkett- und Anschlagkante einen Fd ziehen, die Ränder fest zusammenziehen, an beiden Enden einen Bommel befestigen.

Fifi

quail studio

★ ☆ ☆ ☆

GRÖSSE
Alter

	3-7	9-12	Jahre

YARN
Rowan Soft Bouclé
Schal mit Fransen

	2	2	x 50g

(fotografiert in Snow)

NADELN
Stricknadeln 6 mm

MASCHENPROBE
12 ½ mm und 17 R = 10 x 10 cm, glatt re gestr mit
Ndl Nr. 6 mm.

FERTIGE GRÖSSE
Der Schal ist 12 (14,5) cm breit und 170 (200) cm
lang, ohne Fransen.

SCHAL
15 (18) M mit Ndl Nr. 6 mm anschl.
Mit einer Rechtsr beg und fortlfd glatt re str bis 170
(200) cm erreicht sind, enden mit einer Rückr.
Alle M abk.

FERTIGSTELLUNG
Den Schal dämpfen, siehe Informationsseite.
Fransen
Aus dem Garn 25 (32) cm lange Fäden schneiden
und in Gruppen mit je 6 Fäden in die Anschlag-
und Abkettkante knüpfen. Je Rand werden 6 ((7)
Gruppen mit 6 Fäden in gleichmäßigem Abschnitt
in die Ränder geknüpft.

Teddy
quail studio
★ ★ ☆ ☆

GRÖSSEN

Alter						
	3-4	5-6	7-8	9-10	11-12	Jahre
Brustumfang						
	53-56	59-61	64-66	69-74	76-79	cm
Gestrickter Brustumfang						
	75	80	85	95	100	cm

GARN
Rowan Soft Bouclé

6	6	7	7	8	x 50g

(fotografiert in Biscuit 608 & Snow 600)

NADELN
Stricknadeln 12 mm

MASCHENPROBE
8 M und 12 ½ R = 10 x 10 cm, glatt li gestr mit Ndl Nr. 12 mm und doppeltem Fd.

RÜCKENTEIL
30 (32: 34: 38: 40) M mit Ndl Nr. 12 mm und doppeltem Fd anschl.
Mit einer Linksr beg und fortlfd glatt li str bis 53 (58: 63: 68: 72) cm erreicht sind, enden mit einer Rückr.
Schultern
Am Anf der nächsten 2 R je 10 (10: 11: 12: 13) M abk.
Die restl 10 (12: 12: 14: 14) M abk.

LINKES VORDERTEIL
20 (22: 23: 26: 27) M mit Ndl Nr. 12 mm und doppeltem Fd anschl.
R 1 (Hinr): Li bis zu den letzten 4 M, 4 M re.
R 2: Rechts.
Die 4 M am vord Rand werden weiter kraus re gestr, alle übrigen M glatt li.
Wenn die gleiche Länge erreicht ist wie beim Rückenteil, enden mit einer Rückr.
Schulter
Am Anf der R 10 (10: 11: 12: 13) M abk, wie angegeben str bis zum Ende der R = 10 (12: 12: 14: 14) M für die rückw Halsblende).

Weiterstr bis der Streifen 6 (7,5: 7,5: 9: 9) cm lang ist, enden mit einer Rückr.
Alle M abk.

RECHTES VORDERTEIL
20 (22: 23: 26: 27) M mit Ndl Nr. 12 mm und doppeltem Fd anschl.
R 1 (Hinr): 4 M re, li bis zum Ende.
R 2: Rechts.
Die 4 M am vord Rand werden weiter kraus re gestr, alle übrigen M glatt li.
Das re Vorderteil gegengleich zum li Vorderteil beenden.

ÄRMEL
16 (18: 18: 20: 20) M mit Ndl Nr. 12 mm und doppeltem Fd anschl.
Mit einer Linksr beg und fortlfd glatt li str, dabei für die seitl Zun in der 11. (15.: 11.: 11.: 9.) R und in jeder folg 14. (16.: 12.: 14.: 12.) R bds je 1 M zun bis 20 (22: 24: 26: 28) M erreicht sind.
Nach einer Länge von 25 (29: 33: 37: 42) cm enden mit einer Rückr.
Alle M abk.

FERTIGSTELLUNG
Alle Teile dämpfen, siehe Informationsseite.
Beide Schulternähte schließen.

Die rückw Blenden mit den Abkettkanten zusammennähen und danach an der rückw Halsausschnittkante festnähen.
An allen seitl Rändern von den Schulternähten abwärts je 13 (14: 15: 16,5: 18) cm abmessen und markieren. Die Ärmel mit der Mitte der Abkettkante auf die Schulternähte heften und an den seitl Rändern zwischen den Markierungen festnähen. Die Seiten- und Ärmelnähte schließen.

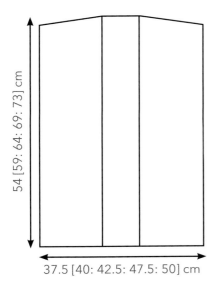

54 [59: 64: 69: 73] cm

37.5 [40: 42.5: 47.5: 50] cm

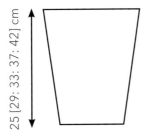

25 [29: 33: 37: 42] cm

Luna

martin storey

★★★☆

GRÖSSEN

Alter						
	3-4	5-6	7-8	9-10	11-12	Jahre
Brustumfang						
	53-56	59-61	64-66	69-74	76-79	cm
Gestrickter Brustumfang						
	69	77	81	87	94	cm

GARN

Rowan Cotton Cashmere

6	6	7	7	8	x 50g

(fotografiert in Pearly Pink 216)

NADELN

Stricknadeln 3 ¼ mm und 3 ¾ mm
Zopfnadel

EXTRAS

Hilfsnadeln
Maschenmarkierer

MASCHENPROBE

31 M und 34 R = 10 x 10 cm, im Mst gestr mit Ndl
Nr. 3 ¾ mm.

SPEZIELLE ABKÜRZUNGEN

Z6H = Die nächsten 3 M auf eine ZN heben und
nach hinten legen, 3 M re, danach die 3 M auf der
ZN re str; **Z6V** = Die nächsten 3 M auf eine ZN
heben und vorne legen, 3 M re, danach die 3 M
auf der ZN re str; **Noppe** = (1 M re, 1 U, 1 M re,
1 U, 1 M re) alle in die nächste M, Arb wenden, 5 M li,
Arb wenden, 5 M re, Arb wenden, übzAbn, 1 M re, 2 M
re zus-str, Arb wenden, 3 M li zus-str, die M wieder
auf die re Ndl heben.

RÜCKENTEIL

107 (119: 125: 135: 145) M mit Ndl Nr. 3 ¼ mm
anschl.
Mit R 1 der Strickschrift wie angegeben beg, die
22 M des Musters werden 4 (4: 5: 5: 5) x je R wdhl,
R 1 und 2 werden 7 (7: 8: 8: 8) x wdhl, enden mit
einer Rückr.
Diese 14 (14: 16: 16: 16) R bilden das
Rippenbündchen.

Wechseln zur Ndl Nr. 3 ¾ mm.
Jetzt R 3-18 fortlfd wdhl bis 37 (41: 45: 49: 52) cm
erreicht sind, enden mit einer Rückr.

Schulterschräge

Am Anf der nächsten 2 (12: 8: 2: 12) R je 3 (4: 4:
4: 5) M abk, danach am Anf der folg 16 (6: 10:
16: 6) R je 4 (5: 5: 5: 6) M abk.
Den Fd abschneiden, die restl 37 (41: 43: 47: 49) M
für die Halsblende auf einer Hilfsndl stilllegen.

VORDERTEIL

Das Vorderteil str wie das Rückenteil bis 4 (6: 6:
6: 8) R unterhalb des Beg der Schulterschrägen,
enden mit einer Rückr.

Vord Halsausschnitt

Nächste R (Hinr): 45 (50: 52: 55: 60) M im Mst, Arb
wenden, die restl M auf einer Hilfsndl stilllegen,
beide Seiten getrennt beenden.
Für die Halsrundung in den nächsten 3 (5: 5: 5: 6) R
je 1 M abn = 42 (45: 47: 50: 54) M.
- (-: -: -: 1) R str, enden mit einer Rückr.

Schulterschräge

Am Anf der nächsten R und - (5: 3: -: 5) x am Anf
jeder folg 2. R je 3 (4: 4: 4: 5) M abk, danach 7 (2:
4: 7: 2) x am Anf jeder folg 2. R je 4 (5: 5: 5: 6) M,
gleichzeitig am Halsausschnitt in den nächsten
3 (1: 1: 1: 1) R je 1 M abn, danach 3 (4: 4: 4: 4) x in
jeder folg 2. R und 1 x in der folg 4. R.

1 R str, danach die restl 4 (5: 5: 5: 6) M abk.
Die stillgelegten M aufn, die mittl 17 (19: 21:
25: 25) M auf einer Hilfsndl stilllegen, mit neuem
Fd in einer Hinr im Mst str bis zum Ende.
Die 2. Seite gegengleich beenden.

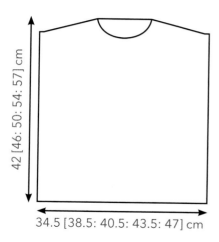

42 [46: 50: 54: 57] cm

34.5 [38.5: 40.5: 43.5: 47] cm

ÄRMEL

51 (55: 55: 59: 59) M mit Ndl Nr. 3 ¼ mm anschl.
Mit R 1 der Strickschrift wie angegeben beg, R 1
und 2 werden 7 (7: 8: 8: 8) x wdhl, enden mit
einer Rückr.
Diese 14 (14: 16: 16: 16) R bildeten das
Rippenbündchen.
Wechseln zur Ndl Nr. 3 ¾ mm.
Jetzt R 3 bis 18 **fortlfd** wdhl, dabei für die seitl Zun
in der 3. R und in jeder folg 4. R bds je 1 M zun bis
75 (69: 87: 97: 105) M erreicht sind, danach - (5: -:
-: -) x in jeder folg 6. R, alle Zun im Musterverlauf
str = 75 (79: 87: 97: 105) M.
Nach einer Länge von 22 (25: 29: 32: 37) cm
enden mit einer Rückr.
Alle M abk.

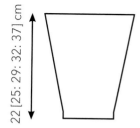

22 [25: 29: 32: 37] cm

FERTIGSTELLUNG

Alle Teile dämpfen, siehe Informationsseite.
Die re SChulternaht schließen.
Halsblende
Von re mit Ndl Nr. 3 ¼ mm die M wie folgt aufn
und re str: Aus der li vord Halsausschnittkante
17 (18: 18: 18: 21) M, die 17 (19: 21: 25: 25) M auf
der Hilfsndl im Vorderteil re str, dabei verteilt 3 M
abn, aus der re vord Halsausschnittkante 17 (18:
18: 18: 21) M, zuletzt die 37 (41: 43: 47: 49) M auf
der Hilfsndl im Rückenteil re str, dabei verteilt 3 M
abn = 82 (90: 94: 102: 110) M.
R 1 (Rückr): 2 M li, *2 M re, 2 M li, ab * wdhl bis
zum Ende.
R 2: 2 M re, *2 M li, 2 M re, ab * wdhl bis zum Ende.
Die 2 R bilden das Rippenmuster, weitere 5 R str,
enden mit einer Rückr.
Die M **sehr locker** im Ripp abk, damit der
Ausschnitt über den Kopf passt.
Die li Schulternaht und die seitl Blendennaht
schließen.
An allen seitl Rändern von den Schulternähten
abwärts je 12 (13: 14: 16,5: 18) cm abmessen
und markieren. Die Ärmel mit der Mitte der
Abkettkante auf die Schulternähte heften und an
den seitl Rändern zwischen den Markierungen
festnähen. Die Seiten- und Ärmelnähte schließen.

Luna Cable Sweater Rücken- und Vorderteil

Legende

☐	Hinr li M, Rückr re M
●	Hinr li M, Rückr re M
○	Umschlag
╱	M re zus-str in der Rückr Noppe
⊡	Noppe
⧓	Z6V
⧓	Z6H

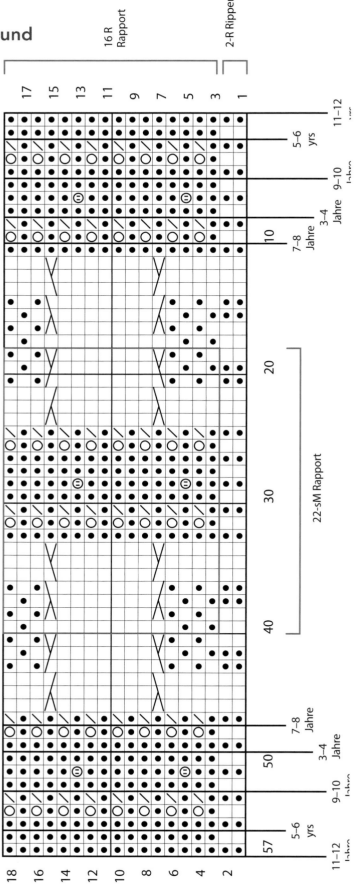

Luna Cable Sweater Ärmel

Legende

☐	Hinr re M, Rückr li M
●	Hinr li M, Rückr re M
⊙	Umschlag
╱	2 M re zus-str in der Rückr
⊕	Noppe
⟩⟨	Z6V
⟨⟩	Z6H

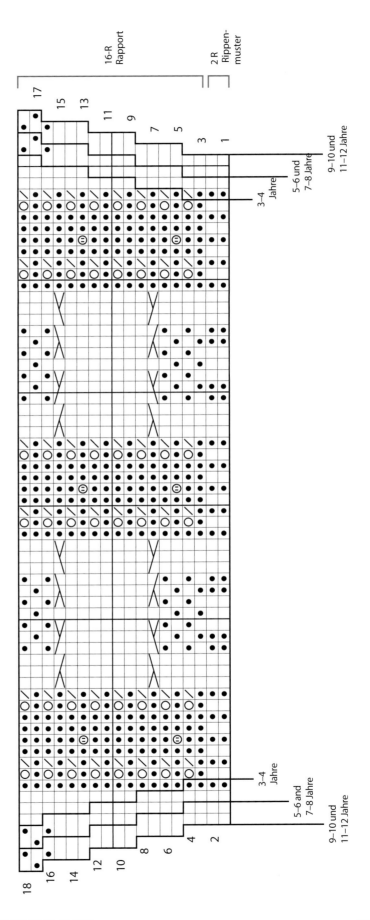

Silver

annika andrea wolke

★ ★ ☆ ☆

GRÖSSEN

Alter

	3-4	5-6	7-8	9-10	11-12	Jahre
Brustumfang						
	53-56	59-61	64-66	69-74	76-79	cm
Gestrickter Brustumfang						
	81	89	94	101	109	cm

GARN

Rowan Alpaca Soft DK and Alpaca Classic

A Alpaca Soft DK | Rainy Day 210

5	5	6	7	8	x 50g

B Alpaca Classic | Feather Grey Melange 101

5	5	6	7	8	x 25g

NADELN

Stricknadeln 5 mm und 6 mm.

EXTRAS

Hilfsnadeln

MASCHENPROBE

16 M und 22 ½ R = 10 x 10 cm, glatt re gestr mit
Ndl Nr. 6 und je einem Fd in Fbe A und B zus
gestr.

RÜCKENTEIL

65 (71: 75: 81: 87) M mit Ndl Nr. 5 mm und je
einem Fd in Fbe A und B zus anschl.
R 1 (RS): 1 M re, *1 M li, 1 M re, ab * wdhl bis zum
Ende.
R 2: 1 M li, *1 M re, 1 M li, ab `wdhl bis zum Ende.
Diese 2 R bilden das Rippenmuster, weitere 6 (6:
8: 8: 8) R str, enden mit einer Rückr.
Wechseln zur Ndl Nr. 6 mm.
Mit einer Rechtsr beg und fortlfd glatt re str bis
45 (50: 55: 58.5: 62) cm erreicht sind, enden mit
einer rückr.

Armausschnitte

Am Anf der nächsten 2 R je 4 (4: 5: 5: 6) M abk =
57 (63: 65: 71: 75) M.
In den nächsten 5 R bds je 1 M abn, danach 3 (5:
5: 6: 6) x in jeder folg 2. R = 41 (43: 45: 49: 53) M.
Nach einer Armausschnittlänge von 13 (14: 15:
16,5: 18) cm enden mit einer Rückr.

Schulterschrägen und rückw Halsausschnitt

Nächste R (Hinr): 5 (5: 5: 6: 7) M abk, re str bis
9 (9: 9: 9: 10) M auf der re Ndl sind, Arb wenden,
die restl M auf einer Hilfsndl stilllegen, beide
Seiten getrennt beenden.
Am Anf der nächsten R 3 M abk.
Die restl 6 (6: 6: 6: 7) M abk.
Die stillgelegten M aufn, mit neuem Fd in einer
Hinr die mittl 13 (15: 17: 19: 19) M abk, re str bis
zum Ende.
Die 2. Seite gegengleich beenden.

LINKES VORDERTEIL

32 (34: 34: 36: 40) M mit Ndl Nr. 5 und je einem Fd
in Fbe A und B zus anschl.
R 1 (Hinr): *1 M re, 1 M li, ab * wdhl bis zu den
letzten 2 M, 2 M re.
R 2: *1 M re, 1 M li, ab * wdhl bis zum Ende.
Weitere 6 (6: 8: 8: 8) R im Ripp str, dabei am Ende
der letzten R 0 (0: 1: 1: 0) M zun, enden mit einer
Rückr = 32 (34: 35: 37: 40) M.
Wechseln zur Ndl Nr. 6 mm.
Nächste R (Hinr): Re bis zu den letzten 9 M, 4 x
(1 M li, 1 M re), 1 M re.
Nächste R: 1 M re, 4 x (1 M li, 1 M re), li bis
zum Ende.
Die 9 M am vord Rand werden weiter im Ripp
gestr, alle übrigen M glatt re.

Gerade str bis die gleiche Länge erreicht ist wie beim Rückenteil vor Beg der Armausschnitte, enden mit einer Rückr.

Armausschnitt
Am Anf der nächsten R 4 (4: 5: 5: 6) M abk = 28 (30: 30: 32: 34) M.
1 R str.
Am Armausschnitt in den nächsten 5 R je 1 M abn, danach 3 (5: 5: 6: 6) x in jeder folg 2. R = 20 (20: 20: 21: 23) M.
Gerade str bis vor Beg der Schulterschräge, enden mit einer Rückr.

Schulterschräge
Am Anf der nächsten R 5 (5: 5: 6: 7) M abk und am Anf der folg 2. R 6 (6: 6: 6: 7) M abk = 9 M.
1 R str, dabei am Ende der R 1 M zun = 10 M.
Die 1. und letzte M in jeder R re str, alle übrigen M im Ripp.
Nach einer Länge von 6 (6,5: 7: 7,5: 7,5) cm alle M im Ripp abk.

RECHTES VORDERTEIL
32 (34: 34: 36: 40) M mit Ndl Nr. 5 und je einem Fd in Fbe A und B zus anschl.
R 1 (Hinr): 2 M re, *1 M li, 1 M re, ab * wdhl bis zum Ende.
R 2: *1 M li, 1 M re, ab * wdhl bis zum Ende.
Weitere 6 (6: 8: 8: 8) R im Ripp str, dabei am Anf der letzten R 0 (0: 1: 1: 0) M zun, enden mit einer Rückr = 32 (34: 35: 37: 40) M.
Wechseln zur Ndl Nr. 6 mm.
Nächste R (Hinr): 1 M re, 4 x (1 M re, 1 M li), re bis zum Ende.
Nächste R: Li bis zu den letzten 9 M, 4 x (1 M re, 1 M li), 1 M re.
Die 9 M am vord Rand werden weiter im Ripp gestr, alle übrigen M glatt re.
Das Mst korrekt einhalten und das re Vorderteil gegengleich zum li Vorderteil beenden.

ÄRMEL
29 (31: 31: 33: 33) M mit Ndl Nr. 5 mm und je einem Fd in Fbe A und B zus anschl.
8 (8: 10: 10: 10) R im Ripp str so wie beim Rückenteil angegeben, enden mit einer Rückr.
Wechseln zur Ndl Nr. 6 mm.
Mit einer Rechtsr beg, fortlfd glatt re str, dabei für die seitl Zun in der 9. (9.: 7.: 7.: 7.) R und in jeder folg 10. (12.: 8.: 8.: 8.) R bds je 1 M zun bis 37 (39: 41: 43: 51) M erreicht sind, danach in jeder folg – (-: 10.: 10.: -) R bis - (-: 43: 47: -) M erreicht sind.
Nach einer Länge von 24 (28: 32: 36: 41) cm enden mit einer Rückr.

Armkugel
Am Anf der nächsten 2 R je 4 (4: 5: 5: 6) M abk = 29 (31: 33: 37: 39) M.
In der nächsten R und 2 x in jeder folg 2. R bds je 1 M abn, danach 1 x in der folg 4. R = 21 (23: 25: 29: 31) M.

1 R str.
In der nächsten R und 2 (1: 2: 2: 3) x in jeder folg 2. R bds je 1 M abn, danach in den folg 3 (5: 5: 7: 7) R, enden mit einer Rückr.
Die restl 9 M abk.

FERTIGSTELLUNG
Alle Teile dämpfen, siehe Informationsseite.
Beide Schulternähte schließen.
Die Halsblenden mit den Abkettkanten zusammennähen und danach an der rückw Halsausschnittkante festnähen.
Die Ärmel in die Armausschnitte nähen, die Seiten- und Ärmelnähte schließen.

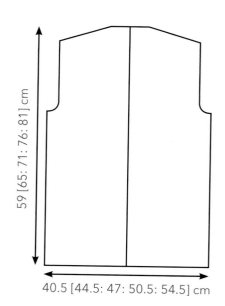

59 [65: 71: 76: 81] cm

40.5 [44.5: 47: 50.5: 54.5] cm

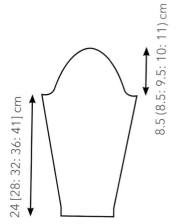

8.5 (8.5: 9.5: 10: 11) cm

24 [28: 32: 36: 41] cm

Moon

lisa richardson

★ ★ ☆ ☆

GRÖSSEN

Alter

	3-6	7-9	10-12	Jahre
Brustumfang				
	53-61	64-69	74-79	cm
Gestrickter Brustumfang, flach liegend				
	64	73	82.5	cm

YARN

Rowan Alpaca Soft DK and Alpaca Classic
A Alpaca Soft DK | Simply White 201

	3	4	5	x 50g
B Alpaca Classic | Snowflake White 115				
	3	4	5	x 25g

NADELN

Stricknadeln 7 mm

MASCHENPROBE

13 M und 25 R = 10 x 10 cm, im Perlmuster gestr mit Ndl Nr. 7 mm und je einem Fd in Fbe A und B zus gestr.

PONCHO

83 (95: 107) M mit Ndl Nr. 7 mm und je einem Fd in Fbe A und B zus anschl.
R 1 (Hinr): 1 M re, *1 M li, 1 M re, ab * wdhl bis zum Ende.
R 2: Wie R 1.
Diese R teilt das Perlmuster ein und wird wdhl bis 30 (34: 38) cm erreicht sind, enden mit einer Rückr.
Halsausschnitt
Nächste R (Hinr): 27 (32: 37) M im Mst, die nächsten 29 (31: 33) M im Mst abk, im Mst str bis zum Ende.
Nächste R: 27 (32: 37) M im Mst, Arb wenden, 29 (31: 33) M anschl, Arb wenden, im Mst str bis zum Ende.
Das Mst korrekt einhalten, gerade str bis 30 (34: 38) cm ab dem Halsausschnitt erreicht sind, danach alle M im Mst abk.

FERTIGSTELLUNG
Den Poncho dämpfen, siehe Informationsseite.

Alaska

quail studio

★ ★ ☆ ☆

GRÖSSEN
Alter

	3-4	5-6	7-8	9-10	11-12	Jahre
Brustumfang						
	53-56	59-61	64-66	69-74	76-79	cm
Gestrickter Brustumfang						
	75	82	88	95	102	cm

GARN
Rowan Alpaca Classic

	9	9	10	11	11	x 25g

(fotografiert in Iced Blue 131)

NADELN
Stricknadeln 5 mm und 6 mm

EXTRAS
Hilfsnadeln

MASCHENPROBE
18 M und 26 R = 10 x 10 cm, kraus re gestr mit Ndl Nr. 6 mm und doppeltem Fd. Die Lochmusterfläche wird über 23 M gestr und ist 12 cm breit.

RÜCKENTEIL
69 (75: 81: 87: 93) M mit Ndl Nr. 5 mm und doppeltem Fd anschl.

R 1 (Hinr): 1 M re, *1 M li, 1 M re, ab * wdhl bis zum Ende.

R 2: 1 M li, *1 M re, 1 M li, ab * wdhl bis zum Ende.
Weitere 6 (6: 6: 8: 8) R im Ripp str, enden mit einer Rückr.
Wechseln zur Ndl Nr. 6 mm und im Mst str wie folgt:

R 1 (Hinr): 8 (10: 13: 15: 18) M re, *8 M re, 2 M re zus-str, 1 U, 1 M re, 1 M li, 1 M re, 1 U, übzAbn, 8 M re*, 7 (9: 9: 11: 11) M re, von * bis *1 x wdhl, 8 (10: 13: 15: 18) M re.

R 2: 8 (10: 13: 15: 18), *7 M li, 2 M li verschr zus-str, 2 M li, 1 U, 1 M re, 1 U, 2 M li, 2 M li zus-str, 7 M li*, 7 (9: 9: 11: 11) M re, von * bis * 1 x wdhl, 8 (10: 13: 15: 18) M re.

R 3: 8 (10: 13: 15: 18) M re, *6 M re, 2 M re zus-str, 1 M re, 1 U, 2 M re, 1 M li, 2 M re, 1 U, 1 M re, übzAbn, 6 M re*, 7 (9: 9: 11: 11) M re, von * bis * 1 x wdhl, 8 (10: 13: 15: 18) M re.

R 4: 8 (10: 13: 15: 18) M re, *5 M li, 2 M li verschr zus-str, 3 M li, 1 U, 1 M li, 1 M re, 1 M li, 1 U, 3 M li, 2 M li zus-str, 5 M li*, 7 (9: 9: 11: 11) M re, von * bis * 1 x wdhl, 8 (10: 13: 15: 18) M re.

R 5: 8 (10: 13: 15: 18) M re, *4 M re, 2 M re zus-str, 2 M re, 1 U, 3 M re, 1 M li, 3 M re, 1 U, 2 M re, übzAbn, 4 M re*, 7 (9: 9: 11: 11) M re, von * bis * 1 x wdhl, 8 (10: 13: 15: 18) M re.

R 6: 8 (10: 13: 15: 18) M re, *3 M li, 2 M li verschr zus-str, 4 M li, 1 U, 2 M li, 1 M re, 2 M li, 1 U, 4 M li, 2 M li zus-str, 3 M li*, 7 (9: 9: 11: 11) M re, von * bis * 1 x wdhl, 8 (10: 13: 15: 18) M re.

R 7: 8 (10: 13: 15: 18) M re, *2 M re, 2 M re zus-str, 3 M re, 1 U, 4 M re, 1 M li, 4 M re, 1 U, 3 M re, übzAbn, 2 M re*, 7 (9: 9: 11: 11) M re, von * bis * 1 x wdhl, 8 (10: 13: 15: 18) M re.

R 8: 8 (10: 13: 15: 18) M re, *1 M li, 2 M li zus-str, 5 M li, 1 U, 3 M li, 1 M re, 3 M li, 1 U, 5 M li, 2 M li zus-str, 1 M li*, 7 (9: 9: 11: 11) M re, von * bis * 1 x wdhl, 8 (10: 13: 15: 18) M re.

R 9: 8 (10: 13: 15: 18) M re, *2 M re zus-str, 4 M re, 1 U, 5 M li, 1 M li, 5 M re, 1 U, 4 M re, übzAbn*, 7 (9: 9: 11: 11) M re, von * bis * 1 x wdhl, 8 (10: 13: 15: 18) M re.

R 10: 8 (10: 13: 15: 18) M re, *11 M li, 1 M re, 11 M li*, 7 (9: 9: 11: 11) M re, von * bis * 1 x wdhl, 8 (10: 13: 15: 18) M re.

R 11: 8 (10: 13: 15: 18) M re, *11 M re, 1 M li, 11 M re*, 7 (9: 9: 11: 11) M re, von * bis * 1 x wdhl, 8 (10: 13: 15: 18) M re.

R 12: Wie R 10.

Diese 12 R bilden das Muster = 2 Musterflächen mit kraus re gestr M dazwischen und an beiden Seiten.

Das Mst korrekt einhalten, nach 28 (31: 34: 36,5: 41) cm enden mit einer Rückr.

Armausschnitte

Am Anf der nächsten 2 R je 2 M abk = 65 (71: 77: 83: 89) M.

Nächste R (Hinr): 2 M re, übzAbn, im Mst bis zu den letzten 4 M, 2 M re zus-str, 2 M re = 63 (69: 75: 81: 87) M.

Alle Abn am Armausschnitt str wie in der letzten R angegeben: In der 2. R und in der folg 2. R bds je 1 M abn = 59 (65: 71: 77: 83) M.

Nach einer Armausschnittlänge von 13 (14: 15: 16,5: 18) cm enden mit einer Rückr.

Schulterschrägen und rückw Halsausschnitt

Nächste R (Hinr): 8 (9: 10: 11: 12) M abk, im Mst str bis 12 (13: 14: 15: 16) M auf der re Ndl sind, Arb wenden, die restl M auf einer Hilfsndl stilllegen, beide Seiten getrennt beenden.

Am Anf der nächsten R 3 M abk.

Die restl 9 (10: 11: 12: 13) M abk.

Die stillgelegten M aufn, die mittl 19 (21: 23: 25: 27) M auf einer Hilfsndl stilllegen, mit neuem Fd in einer Hinr im Mst str bis zum Ende.

Die 2. Seite gegengleich beenden.

VORDERTEIL

Das Vorderteil str wie das Rückenteil bis 14 (16: 16: 16: 18) R unterhalb des Beg der Schulterschrägen, enden mit einer Rückr.

Vord Halsausschnitt

Nächste R (Hinr): 24 (27: 29: 31: 34) M im Mst, Arb wenden, die restl M auf einer Hilfsndl stilllegen, beide Seiten getrennt beenden.

Am Halsausschnitt in den nächsten 4 R je 1 M abn, danach 2 (3: 3: 3: 4) x in jeder folg 2. R und 1 x in der folg 4. R = 17 (19: 21: 23: 25) M.

1 R str, enden mit einer Rückr.

Schulterschräge

Am Anf der nächsten R 8 (9: 10: 11: 12) M abk und am Anf der folg 2. R 9 (10: 11: 12: 13) M.

Die stillgelegten M aufn, die mittl 11 (11: 13: 15: 15) M auf einer Hilfsndl stilllegen, mit neuem Fd in einer Hinr im Mst str bis zum Ende.

Die 2. Seite gegengleich beenden.

ÄRMEL

23 (25: 25: 27: 27) M mit Ndl Nr. 5 und doppeltem Fd anschl.

7 (7: 7: 9: 9) R im Ripp str, so wie beim Rückenteil angegeben, enden mit einer **Hinr.**

Nächste R (Rückr): 1 M li, *in der nächsten M 1 M zun, 1 M li, ab * wdhl bis zum Ende = 34 (37: 37: 40: 40) M.

Wechseln zur Ndl Nr. 6, mit einer Rechtsr beg und fortlfd kraus re str, dabei für die seitl Zun in der

7. (9.: 7.: 7.: 5.) R und in jeder folg 8. (10.: 8.: 8.: 6.) R bds je 1 M zun bis 40 (43: 41: 50: 44) M erreicht sind, danach in jeder folg 10. (12.: 10.: 10.: 8.) R bis 44 (47: 51: 56: 62) M erreicht sind.

Nach einer Länge von 24 (28: 32: 36: 41) cm enden mit einer Rückr.

Armkugel

Am Anf der nächsten 2 R je 2 M abk = 40 (43: 47: 52: 58) M.

Alle seitl Abn str wie bei den Armausschnitten angegeben: In der nächsten R und 1 x in der folg 2. R bds je 1 M abn, danach in der folg R bds je 1 M abn, enden mit einer Rückr.

Die restl 34 (37: 41: 46: 52) M abk.

FERTIGSTELLUNG

Alle Teile dämpfen, siehe Informationsseite.

Die re Schulternaht schließen.

Halsblende

Von re mit Ndl Nr. 5 mm und doppeltem Fd die M wie folgt aufn und re str: Aus der li vord Halsausschnittkante 14 (16: 16: 16: 18) M, die 11 (11: 13: 15: 15) M auf der Hilfsndl im Vorderteil re str, aus der re vord Halsausschnittkante 14 (16: 16: 16: 18) M, aus der re rückw Halsausschnittkante 3 M, die 19 (21: 23: 25: 27) M auf der Hilfsndl im Rückenteil re str, dabei in der Mitte 1 M zun und aus der li rückw Halsausschnittkante 3 M = 65 (71: 75: 79: 85) M.

Mit R 2 des Rippenmusters beg so wie beim Rückenteil angegeben, nach 6 (6: 7: 7: 7) cm alle M **sehr locker** abk, der Ausschnitt muss über den Kopf passen.

Die li Schulternaht und die seitl Blendennaht schließen.

Die Halsblende in der Mitte nach innen umlegen und **locker** festnähen. Die Ärmel in die Armausschnitte nähen, die Seiten- und Ärmelnähte schließen.

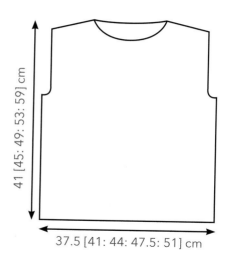

41 [45: 49: 53: 59] cm

37.5 [41: 44: 47.5: 51] cm

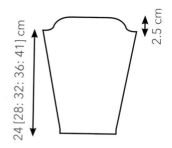

24 [28: 32: 36: 41] cm

2.5 cm

Bear

quail studio

★★☆☆

GRÖSSEN

Alter						
	3-4	5-6	7-8	9-10	11-12	Jahre
Brustumfang						
	53-56	59-61	64-66	69-74	76-79	cm
Gestrickter Brustumfang						
	75	82	88	95	102	cm

GARN

Rowan Soft Bouclé

3	3	4	4	4	x 50g

(fotografiert in Shrimp 601 & Natural 602)

NADELN

Stricknadeln 6 mm

EXTRAS

Maschenmarkierer (Mm)

MASCHENPROBE

12 M und 18 R = 10 x 10 cm, im Perlmuster gestr
mit Ndl Nr. 6 mm.

RÜCKENTEIL

45 (49: 53: 57: 61) M mit Ndl Nr. 6 mm anschl.
R 1 (Hinr): 1 M re, *1 M li, 1 M re, ab * wdhl bis zum
Ende.
R 2: Wie R 1.
Diese 2 R bilden das Perlmuster und werden wdhl
bis 39 (44: 48: 52: 54) cm erreicht sind, enden mit
einer Rückr.

Armausschnitte

Am Anf der nächsten 2 R je 2 (3: 3: 4: 4) M abk =
41 (43: 47: 49: 53) M.
Am Armausschnitt in den nächsten 3 R bds je 1 M
abn, danach 2 (2: 3: 3: 4) x in jeder folg 2. R = 31
(33: 35: 37: 39) M.
Nach einer Armausschnittlänge von 15 (16: 17:
19: 21) cm enden mit einer Rückr.

Schulterschrägen

Am Anf der nächsten 2 R je 3 (4: 4: 4: 4) M abk,
und am Anf der nächsten 2 R je 4 (4: 4: 4: 5) M.
Die restl 17 (17: 19: 21: 21) M abk.

LINKES VORDERTEIL

27 (29: 31: 33: 35) M mit Ndl Nr. 6 mm anschl.
Im Perlmuster str bis das Vorderteil so lang ist wie
das Rückenteil vor Beg der Armausschnitte, enden
mit einer Rückr.

Armausschnitt

Am Anf der nächsten R 2 (3: 3: 4: 4) M abk =
25 (26: 28: 29: 31) M.
1 R str, enden mit einer Rückr.

Vord Schräge

In der letzten R nach der 4. M ab dem vord Rand
einen Mm platzieren (für die Bruchlinie des
Besatzes).
Nächste R (Hinr): 2 M zus-str (Abn für den
Armausschnitt), im Perlmuster bis 2 M vor der mark
M, 2 M zus-str (Abn für die vord Schräge), den
Mm abheben, 2 M zus-str (Abn für den Besatz),
1 M im Perlmuster, in der letzten M 1 M zun (Zun
als Ausgleich für die Abn nach dem Mm, für den
Besatz befinden sich ab dem Mm immer 4 M bis
zum vord Rand auf der Ndl) = 23 (24: 26: 27: 29) M.
Alle Ab- und Zun am vord Rand str wie in der
letzten R angegeben: Am Armausschnitt in den
nächsten 2 R je 1 M abn, danach 2 (2: 3: 3: 4) x in
jeder folg 2. R, **gleichzeitig** am vord Rand in der 2.
R und 2 (2: 3: 3: 4) x in jeder folg 2. R je 1 M abn =
16 (17: 17: 18: 18) M.
Nur noch am vord Rand in der 2. (2.: 2.: 2.: 4.) R

und 2 (2: 2: 2: 0) x in jeder folg 2. R je 1 M abn, danach 2 (2: 2: 3: 4) x in jeder folg 4. R = 11 (12: 12: 12: 13) M.
Gerade str bis das Vorderteil so lang ist wie das Rückenteil vor Beg der Armausschnitte, enden mit einer Rückr.

Schulterschräge
Am Anf der nächsten R 3 (4: 4: 4: 4) M abk und am Anf der folg 2. R 4 (4: 4: 4: 5) M = 4 M.
1 R str, dabei am Ende der R 1 M zun = 5 M.
Weiter im Perlmuster str bis der Streifen für den rückw Besatz 7 (7: 8: 8,5: 8,5) cm lang ist, enden mit einer Rückr.
Die M abk.

RECHTES VORDERTEIL
27 (29: 31: 33: 35) M mit Ndl Nr. 6 mm anschl.
Im Perlmuster str bis das Vorderteil so lang ist wie das Rückenteil vor Beg der Armausschnitte, enden mit einer Rückr.

Armausschnitt
1 R str.
Am Anf der nächsten R 2 (3: 3: 4: 4) M abk = 25 (26: 28: 29: 31) M.

Vord Schräge
In der letzten R nach der 4. M ab dem vord Rand einen Mm platzieren (für die Bruchlinie des Besatzes).
Nächste R (Hinr): In der 1. M 1 M zun (Zun als Ausgleich für die Abn nach dem Mm, für den Besatz befinden sich ab dem Mm immer 4 M bis zum vord Rand auf der Ndl), 1 M im Mst, 2 M zus-str, den Mm abheben, im Mst bis zu den letzten 2 M, 2 M zus-str (Abn für den Armausschnitt = 23 (24: 26: 27: 29) M.
Alle Ab- und Zun am vord Rand str wie in der letzten R angegeben und das re Vorderteil gegengleich zum li Vorderteil beenden.

FERTIGSTELLUNG
Alle Teile dämpfen, siehe Informationsseite.
Beide Schulternähte schließen.
Die rückw Besätze mit den Abkettkanten zusammennähen, danach den Rand an seitl Rand an der rückw Halsausschnittkante festnähen.
Die 4 M des Besatzes nach innen umlegen und festnähen.
Die Seitennähte schließen.

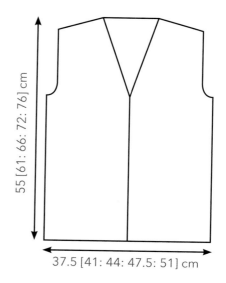

55 [61: 66: 72: 76] cm

37.5 [41: 44: 47.5: 51] cm

Ivy
chloe thurlow
★★☆☆

GRÖSSEN

Alter						
	3-4	5-6	7-8	9-10	11-12	Jahre
Brustumfang						
	53-56	59-61	64-66	69-74	76-79	cm
Gestrickter Brustumfang						
	64	70	74	80	86	cm

GARN
Rowan Handknit Cotton

A Iced Water 239						
	4	4	5	5	6	x 50g
B Bleached 263						
	1	1	1	1	1	x 50g

NADELN
Stricknadeln 3 ¼ mm und 4 mm
1 Rundstrickndl 3 ¼ mm, höchstens 50 (50: 60: 70: 70) cm lang

EXTRAS
Hilfsnadeln

MASCHENPROBE
20 M und 30 R = 10 x 10 cm, glatt re gestr mit Ndl Nr. 4 mm.

RÜCKENTEIL
63 (69: 73: 79: 85) M mit Ndl Nr. 3 ¼ mm und Fbe A anschl.
R 1 (Hinr): 1 M re, *1 M li, 1 M re, ab * wdhl bis zum Ende.
R 2: 1 M li, *1 M re, 1 M li, ab * wdhl bis zum Ende.
Diese 2 R bilden das Rippenmuster, weitere 4 (4: 6: 6: 6) R str, dabei am Ende der letzten R 1 M zun, enden mit einer Rückr = 64 (70: 74: 80: 86) M.
Wechseln zur Ndl Nr. 4 mm.
Mit einer Rechtsr beg und fortlfd glatt re im Streifenmuster str wie folgt:
Mit Fbe A 8 (8: 10: 10: 12) R, danach mit Fbe B 2 R.
Diese 10 (10: 12: 12: 14) R bilden das Streifenmuster und werden fortlfd wdhl. **
Weiter glatt re str bis 14 (16: 17: 19: 20) cm erreicht sind, enden mit einer Rückr.
Rückw Halsausschnitt
Nächste R (Hinr): 32 (35: 37: 40: 43) M re, Arb wenden, die restl M auf einer Hilfsndl stilllegen, beide Seiten getrennt beenden.
1 R str, enden mit einer Rückr.
Nächste R (Hinr): Re str bis zu den letzten 4 M, 2 M re zus-str, 2 M re = 31 (34: 36: 39: 42) M.

Alle Abn am Halsausschnitt str wie in der letzten R angegeben: In der 2. R und 3 (4: 3: 2: 5) x in jeder folg 2. R je 1 M abn, danach 11 (12: 14: 16: 15) x in jeder folg 4. R = 16 (17: 18: 20: 21) M.
5 R str, enden mit einer Rückr.
Schulterschräge
Am Anf der nächsten R und am Anf der folg 2. R je 5 (6: 6: 7: 7) M abk.
1 R str, danach die restl 6 (5: 6: 6: 7) M abk.
Die stillgelegten M aufn, mit neuem Fd in einer Hinr re str bis zum Ende.
1 R str.
Nächste R (Hinr): 2 M re, übzAbn, re bis zum Ende.
Alle Abn am Halsausschnitt str wie in der letzten R angegeben und die 2. Seite gegengleich beenden.

VORDERTEIL
Das Vorderteil str wie das Rückenteil, angegeben bis **.
Das Mst korrekt einhalten bis 2 R unterhalb des Beg der Schulterschrägen, enden mit einer Rückr.
Vord Halsausschnitt
Nächste R (Hinr): 21 (22: 23: 25: 26) M re, Arb wenden, die restl M auf einer Hilfsndl stilllegen, beide Seiten getrennt beenden.
Am Halsausschnitt in der nächsten R 1 M abn = 20 (21: 22: 24: 25) M.
Schulterschräge
Am Halsausschnitt in den nächsten 4 R je 1 M abn, enden mit einer Rückr, **gleichzeitig** am Anf der

nächsten R und am Anf der folg 2. R je 5 (6: 6: 7: 7) M abk.

Die restl 6 (5: 6: 6: 7) M.

Die stillgelegten M aufn, die mittl 22 (26: 28: 30: 34) M auf einer Hilfsndl stilllegen, mit neuem Fd in einer Hinr re str bis zum Ende.

Die 2. Seite gegengleich beenden.

FERTIGSTELLUNG
Alle Teile dämpfen, siehe Informationsseite.
Beide Schulternähte schließen.

Halsblende
Von re mit der Rundstrickndl Nr. 3 ¼ mm und Fbe A aus der li vord Halsausschnittkante 5 M aufn und re str, die 22 (26: 28: 30: 34) M auf der Hilfsndl im Vorderteil re str, dabei in der Mitte 1 M zun, aus der re vord Halsausschnittkante 5 M aufn und re str, aus der re rückw Halsausschnittkante 52 (56: 60: 66: 68) M aufn und re str, aus der unteren Spitze des V's 1 M aufn und re str, diese M mit einem Kontrastfaden markieren und aus der li rückw Halsausschnittkante 52 (56: 60: 66: 68) M aufn und re str = 138 (150: 160: 176: 182) M.
In Runden str wie folgt, dabei Anf und Ende jeder Rde markieren:

Rde 1 (Hinr): *1 M re, 1 M li, ab * wdhl bis 3 M vor der mark M, 1 M re, 2 M re zus-str, die mark M li str, übzAbn, **1 M re, 1 M li, ab ** wdhl bis zum Ende. Das Rippenmuster korrekt einhalten wie folgt:

Rde 2: Im Ripp bis 2 M vor der mark M, 2 M re zus-str, die mark M li str, übzAbn, im Ripp bis zum Ende.

Die letzte Rde noch 5 x wdhl = 124 (136: 146: 162: 168) M.

Alle M im Ripp abk, dabei die Abn bds der mark M noch 1 x wdhl.

An allen seitl Rändern von den Schulternähten abwärts je 14 (15: 16,5: 18: 20) cm abmessen und markieren.

Armausschnittblenden (beide gleich)
Von re mit Ndl Nr. 3 ¼ mm und Fbe A aus der ganzen Armausschnittkante zwischen den Markierungen 55 (59: 65: 71: 79) M aufn und re str. Mit R 2 des Rippenmusters beg so wie beim Rückenteil angegeben, nach 7 R alle M im Ripp abk.

Die Seitennähte schließen.

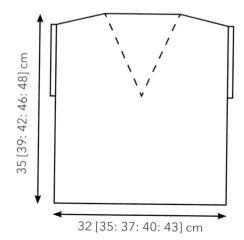

35 [39: 42: 46: 48] cm

32 [35: 37: 40: 43] cm

Cub
quail studio
★ ☆ ☆ ☆

GRÖSSEN
Alter

	3-4	5-6	7-8	9-10	11-12	Jahre
Brustumfang		53-56	59-61	64-66	69-74	76-79	cm
Gestrickter Brustumfang		75	82	88	94	100	cm

GARN
Rowan Brushed Fleece

4	4	4	5	5	x 50g

(fotografiert in Cove 251 & Cairn 263)

NADELN
1 pair 5½mm (no 5) (US 9) needles
1 pair 6mm (no 4) (US 10) needles

EXTRAS
Hilfsnadeln

MASCHENPROBE
13 M und 19 R = 10 x 10 cm, glatt re gestr mit Ndl Nr. 6 mm.

RÜCKENTEIL
49 (53: 57: 61: 65) M mit Ndl Nr. 5 ½ mm anschl.
R 1 (Hinr): 1 (0: 0: 2: 0) M re, 2 (0: 2: 2: 1) M li, *3 M re, 2 M li, ab * wdhl bis zu den letzten 1 (3: 0: 2: 4) M, 1 (3: 0: 2: 3) M re, 0 (0: 0: 0: 1) M li.
R 2: 1 (0: 0: 2: 0) M li, 2 (0: 2: 2: 1) M re, *3 M li, 2 M re, ab * wdhl bis zu den letzten 1 (3: 0: 2: 4) M, 1 (3: 0: 2: 3) M li, 0 (0: 0: 0: 1) M re.
Diese 2 R bilden das Rippenmuster und werden wdhl bis 6 (7: 7: 8: 8) cm erreicht sind, enden mit einer Rückr.
Wechseln zur Ndl Nr. 6 mm, mit einer Rechtsr beg und fortlfd glatt re str bis 27,5 (31: 34: 36: 37,5) cm erreicht sind, enden mit einer Rückr.
Armausschnitte
Am Anf der nächsten 2 R je 2 M abk = 45 (49: 53: 57: 61) M.
Für die Armausschnittrundungen in der nächsten R und 1 x in der folg 2. R bds je 1 M abn = 41 (45: 49: 53: 57) M.
Nach einer Armausschnittlänge von 15,5 (17: 18: 20: 21,5) cm enden mit einer Rückr.
Schulterschrägen und rückw Halsausschnitt
Nächste R (Hinr): 6 (7: 7: 8: 9) M abk, re str bis 9 (10: 11: 11: 12) M auf der re Ndl sind, Arb

wenden, die restl M auf einer Hilfsndl stilllegen, beide Seiten getrennt beenden.
Am Anf der nächsten R 3 M abk.
Die restl 6 (7: 8: 8: 9) M abk.
Die stillgelegten M aufn, die mittl 11 (11: 13: 15: 15) M auf einer Hilfsndl stilllegen, mit neuem Fd in einer Hinr re str bis zum Ende.
Die 2. Seite gegengleich beenden.

VORDERTEIL
Das Vorderteil str wie das Rückenteil bis 6 (8: 8: 8: 10) R unterhalb des Beg der Schulterschrägen, enden mit einer Rückr.
Vord Halsausschnitt
Nächste R (RS): 15 (18: 19: 20: 23) M re, Arb wenden, die restl M auf einer Hilfsndl stilllegen, beide Seiten getrennt beenden.
Für die Halsrundung in den nächsten 2 R je 1 M abn, danach 1 (2: 2: 2: 3) x in jeder folg 2. R = 12 (14: 15: 16: 18) M.
1 R str, enden mit einer Rückr.
Schulterschräge
Am Anf der nächsten R 6 (7: 7: 8: 9) M abk und am Anf der folg 2. R 6 (7: 8: 8: 9) M.
Die stillgelegten M aufn, die mittl 11 (9: 11: 13: 11) M auf einer Hilfsndl stilllegen, mit neuem Fd in einer Hinr re str bis zum Ende.
Die 2. Seite gegengleich beenden.

ÄRMEL

25 (27: 27: 29: 29) M mit Ndl Nr. 5 ½ mm anschl.

R 1 (Hinr): 0 (0: 0: 1: 1) M re, 1 (2: 2: 2: 2) M li, *3 M re,
2 M li, ab * wdhl bis zu den letzten 4 (0: 0: 1: 1) M,
3 (0: 0: 1: 1) M re, 1 (0: 0: 0: 0) M li.

R 2: 0 (0: 0: 1: 1) M li, 1 (2: 2: 2: 2) M re, *3 M li,
2 M re, ab * wdhl bis zu den letzten 4 (0: 0: 1: 1) M,
3 (0: 0: 1: 1) M li, 1 (0: 0: 0: 0) M re.

Weiter im Ripp str bis 4 (5: 5: 6: 6) cm erreicht
sind, enden mit einer Rückr.

Wechseln zur Ndl Nr. 6 mm.

Mit einer Rechtsr beg und fortlfd glatt re str, nach
2 R enden mit einer Rückr.

Nächste R (Hinr): 2 M re, 1 M zun, re bis zu den
letzten 2 M, 1 M zun, 2 M re = 27 (29: 29: 31: 31) M.
Alle seitl Zun str wie in der letzten R angegeben:
In der 4. R und und in jeder folg 4. R bds je 1 M
zun bis 31 (33: 37: 41: 43) M erreicht sind, danach
in jeder folg 6. R bis 37 (41: 45: 49: 53) M erreicht
sind.

Nach einer Länge von 24 (28: 32: 36: 41) cm
enden mit einer Rückr.

Armkugel

Am Anf der nächsten 2 R je 2 M abk = 33 (37: 41:
45: 49) M.

In den nächsten 2 R bds je 1 M abn.

Die restl 29 (33: 37: 41: 45) M abk.

FERTIGSTELLUNG

Alle Teile dämpfen, siehe Informationsseite.
Die re Schulternaht schließen.

Halsblende

Von re mit Ndl Nr. 5 ½ mm die M wie folgt aufn
und re str: Aus der li vord Halsausschnittkante
7 (8: 8: 9: 10) M, die 11 (9: 11: 13: 11) M auf
der Hilfsndl im Vorderteil re str, aus der re vord
Halsausschnittkante 7 (8: 8: 9: 10) M, aus der re
rückw Halsausschnittkante 3 M, die 11 (11: 13:
15: 15) M auf der Hilfsndl im Rückenteil re str,
dabei in der Mitte 0 (0: 1: 0: 0) M zun, und aus der
li rückw Halsausschnittkante 3 M = 42 (42: 47:
52: 52) M.

R 1 (Rückr): 2 M re, *3 M li, 2 M re, ab * wdhl bis
zum Ende.

R 2: 2 M li, *3 M re, 2 M li, ab * wdhl bis zum Ende.

Weiter im Ripp str bis 6 (7: 7: 8: 8) cm erreicht
sind, enden mit einer Rückr.

Alle M **sehr locker** im Ripp abk, der Ausschnitt
muss über den Kopf passen.

Die li Schulternaht und die seitl Blendennaht
schließen.

Die Ärmel in die Armausschnitte nähen, die Seiten-
und Ärmelnähte schließen.

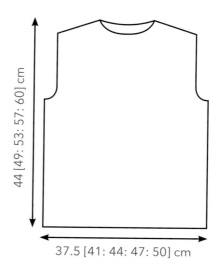

44 [49: 53: 57: 60] cm

37.5 [41: 44: 47: 50] cm

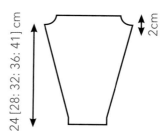

24 [28: 32: 36: 41] cm

2 cm

Haze

quail studio

★★★☆

GRÖSSEN

Alter					
	3-4	5-6	7-8	9-10	11-12	Jahre
Brustumfang					
	53-56	59-61	64-66	69-74	76-79	cm
Gestrickter Brustumfang					
	68	75	78	85	92	cm

GARN

Rowan Big Wool

8	9	10	10	11	x 100g

(fotografiert in Prize 64)

NADELN

Stricknadeln 8 mm
1 Rundstrickndl 8 mm, mindestens 80 (90: 100: 110: 120) cm lang.

EXTRAS

Hilfsnadeln
Maschenmarkierer

MASCHENPROBE

12 M und 26 R = 10 x 10 cm, kraus re gestr mit Ndl
Nr. 8 mm.

SPEZIELLE ABKÜRZUNG

Noppe = Je 1 x im Wechsel von vorne, von hinten,
von vorne und wieder von hinten in die nächste M
einstechen und je eine M re str, diese 4 M wieder
auf die li Ndl heben, 4 M re, dabei den Fd über
die Rückseite wieder auf re Seite holen, 4 M re, die
4., 3. und 2. M auf der re Ndl über die 1. M heben
und von der re Ndl fallen lassen.

RÜCKENTEIL

41 (47: 47: 53: 56) M mit Ndl Nr. 8 mm anschl.
R 1 (Hinr): 2 M li, *1 M re, 2 M li, ab * wdhl bis
zum Ende.
R 2: 2 M re, *1 M li, 2 M re, ab * wdhl bis zum Ende.
Die 2 R bilden das Rippenmuster, weitere 4 (4: 6:
6: 6) R str, dabei in der letzten R verteilt - (2: -: 2: 1)
M abn, enden mit einer Rückr = 41 (45: 47:
51: 55) M.
Mit einer Rechtsr beg und fortlfd kraus re str bis
53 (58: 63: 68: 72) cm erreicht sind, enden mit
einer Rückr.
Schulterschrägen
Am Anf der nächsten 2 R je 6 (6: 6: 7: 7) M abk,
und am Anf der folg 2 R je 6 (7: 7: 7: 8) M abk.
Den Fd abschneiden, die restl 17 (19: 21: 23: 25) M
auf einer Hilfsndl stilllegen.

LINKES VORDERTEIL

14 (14: 14: 14: 17) M mit Ndl Nr. 8 mm anschl.
6 (6: 8: 8: 8) R im Ripp str, so wie beim Rückenteil
angegeben, dabei in der letzten R verteilt 2 (1: 1:
-: 2) M abn, enden mit einer Rückr = 12 (13: 13:
14: 15) M.
Mit einer Rechtsr beg und fortlfd kraus re str bis
dieselbe Länge erreicht ist wie beim Rückenteil vor
Beg der Schulterschrägen, enden mit einer Rückr.
Schulterschräge
Am Anf der nächsten R 6 (6: 6: 7: 7) M abk und am
Anf der folg 2. R die restl 6 (7: 7: 7: 8) M abk.

RECHTES VORDERTEIL

Str wie das li Vorderteil, alle Abn gegengleich str.

ÄRMEL

23 (23: 23: 26: 26) M mit Ndl Nr. 8 mm anschl.
6 (6: 8: 8: 8) R im Ripp str, dabei in der letzten R
verteilt 0 (2: 2: 1: 1) M zun, enden mit einer Rückr
= 23 (25: 25: 27: 27) M.
Im Noppenmuster str wie folgt:
R 1 (Hinr): 3 (4: 4: 1: 1) M re, Noppe, *3 M re,
Noppe, ab * wdhl bis zu den letzten 3 (4: 4: 1: 1) M,
3 (4: 4: 1: 1) M re.
R 2: Links.
R 3: 1 (2: 2: 3: 3) M re, Noppe, *3 M re, Noppe, ab
* wdhl bis zu den letzten 1 (2: 2: 3: 3) M, 1 (2: 2:
3: 3) M re.
R 4: Links.
Diese 4 R bilden das Noppenmuster, weitere
6 R str, dabei in der 3. R bds je 1 M zun, alle Zun im
Musterverlauf str, enden mit einer Rückr = 25 (27:
27: 29: 29) M.

Weiter kraus re str, dabei für die seitl Zun in der 5. R und in jeder folg 8. R bds je 1 M zun bis 33 (35: 37: 39: 47) M erreicht sind, danach - (1: 1: 2: -) x in jeder folg 10. R = - (37: 39: 43: -) M.
Nach einer Länge von 23 (27: 31: 37: 40) cm, enden mit einer Rückr.
Alle M abk.

FERTIGSTELLUNG
Alle Teile dämpfen, siehe Informationsseite.
Beide Schulternähte schließen.
Vorderteilblende
Von re mit der Rundstrickndl Nr. 8 mm die M wie folgt aufn und re str, beg und enden an den Anschlagkanten der Vorderteile:
Aus der re Vorderteilkante bis zur Schulter 65 (70: 77: 83: 88) M, die 17 (19: 21: 23: 25) M auf der Hilfsndl im Rückenteil re str, dabei in der Mitte 1 (1: 0: 1: 1) M zun und aus der li Vorderteilkante 65 (70: 77: 83: 88) M = 148 (160: 175: 190: 202) M.

R 1 (Rückr): Rechts.
R 2: Rechts.
R 3: 1 M re, *2 M li, 1 M re, ab * wdhl bis zum Ende.
R 4: 1 M li, *2 M re, 1 M li, ab * wdhl bis zum Ende.
Weiter im Ripp str bis 6 (6: 7: 7: 7) cm erreicht sind, enden mit einer Rückr.
Alle M im Ripp abk.
An allen seitl Rändern von den Schulternähten abwärts je 14 (16: 17: 18: 20) cm abmessen und markieren. Die Ärmel mit der Mitte der Abkettkante auf die Schulternähte heften und an den seitl Rändern zwischen den Markierungen festnähen. Die Seiten- und Ärmelnähte schließen.

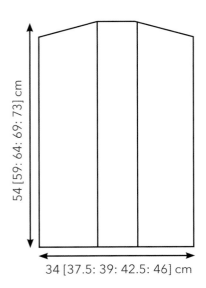

54 [59: 64: 69: 73] cm

34 [37.5: 39: 42.5: 46] cm

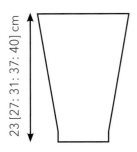

23 [27: 31: 37: 40] cm

Rosie
quail studio
★ ☆ ☆ ☆

GRÖSSE
Alter

	3-7	9-12	Jahre
Kopfumfang (nicht gedehnt)			
	41	46	cm

GARN
Rowan Big Wool

	1	1	x 100g

(fotografiert in Prize 64 & Ice Blue 21)

NADELN
Stricknadeln 7 mm

EXTRAS – 1 Bommel, gekauft (optional)

MASCHENPROBE
12 M und 24 R = 10 x 10 cm, kraus re gestr mit Ndl Nr. 7 mm.

MÜTZE
49 (55) M mit Ndl Nr. 7 mm anschl.
R 1 (RS): 1 M re, *1 M li, 1 M re, ab * wdhl bis zum Ende.
R 2: 1 M li, *1 M re, 1 M li, ab * wdhl bis zum Ende.
Die 2 R bilden das Rippenmuster, weitere 6 (8) R str, enden mit einer Rückr.
Weiter kraus re str bis 15 (16) cm erreicht sind, enden mit einer Rückr.
Spitze
R 1 (Hinr): 8 (9) x (4 M re, 2 M re zus-str), 1 M re = 41 (46) M.
3 R str.
R 5: 8 (9) x (3 M re, 2 M re zus-str), 1 M re = 33 (37) M.
1 R str.
R 7: 8 (9) x (2 M re, 2 M re zus-str), 1 M re = 25 (28) M.
1 R str.
R 9: 8 (9) x (1 M re, 2 M re zus-str), 1 M re = 17 (19) M.
1 R str.
R 11: 8 (9) x (2 M re zus-str), 1 M re = 9 (10) M.
1 R str, enden mit einer Rückr.
Den Fd abschneiden und durch die restl M ziehen, die 9 (10) M fest zusammenziehen, den Fd gut vernähen.

FERTIGSTELLUNG
Die Mütze dämpfen, siehe Informationsseite. Den Bommel auf der Mütze festnähen (falls erwünscht).

Maschenprobe

Die Einhaltung der richtigen Maschenprobe ist wahrscheinlich der wichtigste Faktor, der den Unterschied zwischen einem gelungenen Meisterwerk und einem verpatzten Kleidungsstück ausmacht. Form und Größe, aber auch Fall und Sitz des Gestrickten hängen von ihr ab, daher können bereits kleinste Abweichungen die Gesamtwirkung zerstören.

Am Anfang jeder Anleitung steht die tatsächliche Maschenprobe des Designers und diese müssen Sie einhalten. Es kann sogar sein, daß für ein Strickstück mehrere Maschenproben genannt werden, wenn Teile der Arbeit in Intarsientechnik, andere Teile glatt rechts und wieder andere in Jacquard-Technik gestrickt sind. Wir raten Ihnen dringend eine Strickprobe im jeweiligen Muster zu stricken, die 5-10 Maschen breiter und 5-10 Reihen länger ist als in der Maschenprobe angegeben. Legen Sie diese Strickprobe flach auf den Tisch und messen Sie sie in ihrer Mitte ab. Wenn Sie zu viele Maschen auf 10 cm zählen, stricken Sie eine neue Maschenprobe, bei der Sie dickere Nadeln verwenden. Zählen Sie weniger Maschen auf 10 cm, versuchen Sie es noch einmal mit dünneren Nadeln. Die Angaben über Nadelstärken in den Anleitungen sind nur sehr ungenaue Orientierungshilfen, da jeder eine andere Fadenspannung hat und die Maschen dadurch von Person zu Person unterschiedlich groß werden.

Größen

Bei vielen Anleitungen sind mehrere Größen angegeben. Steht nur eine Zahl da, gilt sie für alle Größen, sind mehrere Zahlen hintereinander angegeben, gilt die erste für die kleinste Größe und die restlichen in Klammern jeweils für die dann folgenden größeren Größen. Die kleine Schnittzeichnung am Ende jeder Anleitung zeigt die fertig gestrickten Maße, außerdem finden Sie eine genaue Größentabelle auf der vorherigen Seite.

Zählmuster

Einige der Modelle in diesem Heft werden nach einem Zählmuster gearbeitet. Darin steht jedes Kästchen für eine Masche und jede Kästchenreihe für eine Strickreihe. Beim Stricken nach den Zählmustern werden die Hinreihen von rechts nach links gelesen und gestrickt, die Rückreihen von links nach rechts, falls nicht anders angegeben. Jede verwendete Farbe ist durch ein eigenes Symbol oder einen eigenen Buchstaben gekennzeichnet. Zur Erleichterung der Arbeit können Sie das Diagramm vergrößert fotokopieren und die benötigte Größe, auch im Text, farbig markieren.

Lochmuster

Beim Lochmuster müssen immer ebenso viele Umschläge gestrickt werden, wie Maschen zusammen gestrickt werden. Sollten, bedingt durch die seitlichen Ab- oder Zunahmen für die Formgebung an den Rändern nicht mehr genügend Maschen für eine vollständige Musterfolge vorhanden sein, werden die restlichen Maschen solange glatt rechts gestrickt, bis wieder genug Maschen für eine Musterfolge vorhanden sind. Eine Hilfe ist es, links und rechts des vollständigen Musters je einen Markierungsring einzuhängen.

Stricken mit Farben

Für das Arbeiten mit Fraben gibt es zwei Haupttechniken: Intarsientechnik und Norweger- oder Fair-Isle Technik. Mit der ersten Technik erhalten Sie einen einlagigen Stoff und sie wird nur dann verwendet, wenn Farbe an einer bestimmten Stelle gestrickt wird. Die Norweger- oder Fair-Isle Technik hingegen produziert einen dickeren Stoff, da mehr als eine Farbe durchgehend über die ganze Reihe gestrickt wird.

Intarsientechnik

Am einfachsten geht es, wenn man für jedes Motiv oder für jedes Farbfeld kürzere Fäden der benötigten Farben abschneidet (je nach Größe des Motivs 50 cm bis 3 m lange Fäden, die auf der Rückseite hängen bleiben, wenn sie nicht benötigt werden), – so verhindert man, dass sich die Knäuel verknoten. Bei jedem Farbwechsel innerhalb der Reihe werden die Fäden miteinander verkreuzt, damit keine Löcher entstehen. Die Enden der Fäden können am Schluss entlang der Farbwechsel vernäht oder beim Stricken "eingewebt" werden. Das Einweben erfolgt nach dem gleichen Prinzip wie das Einweben bei der Norwegertechnik, und erspart das zeitraubende Vernähen der Fäden. Bei der Intarsientechnik ist zu beachten, dass die Maschenprobe von einer glatt rechts gestrickten einfarbigen Maschenprobe abweichen kann.

Norweger- oder Fair-Isle Technik

Wenn zwei oder drei Farben im Laufe einer Reihe ständig wiederholt werden, nehmen Sie den oder die gerade nicht benötigten Fäden locker gespannt auf der Rückseite der Arbeit mit. Wenn Sie mit mehr als zwei Farben arbeiten, behandeln Sie die mitgeführten Fäden wie einen einzigen Faden und dehnen Sie die Maschen immer wieder auf ihre richtige Weite aus, damit die Fäden locker genug, aber nicht zu locker hängen. Spannen Sie die mitgeführten Fäden nie über mehr als drei Maschen, sondern geben Sie den Spannfäden Halt, indem Sie sie bei jeder 2. oder 3. Masche einweben, d. h. umfassen Sie sie abwechselnd unter und über dem Arbeitsfaden. Dadurch werden sie auf der Rückseite der Arbeit festgehalten.

Fertigstellung

Nachdem so viele Stunden an einem Strickstück gestrickt wurde, ist es schade, dass so viele Modelle durch die falsche Behandlung beim Bügeln verdorben werden. Hier einige Tipps für eine wirklich perfekte Konfektionierung.

Dämpfen

Nach Abschluss der Arbeit werden alle Fäden vernäht und alle Strickteile einzeln auf einer weichen Unterlage mit rostfreien Stecknadeln aufgesteckt (oberhalb der eventuellen Rippenmusterbereiche) und mit einem feuchten Tuch bedeckt. Wenn das Tuch trocken ist, ist die Arbeit auf sanfte Art in Form gebracht, ohne dabei ihr Volumen und ihre lebendige Struktur zu verlieren, wie das beim vielfach empfohlenen Bügeln unter einem feuchten Tuch leicht der Fall ist. Beachten Sie auch immer die Hinweise auf der Banderole.

Zusammennähen

Beim Zusammennähen der Teile achten Sie auf genaue Übereinstimmung der Farben. Sie können die Teile sehr sorgfältig von links mit Steppstichen (besonders Armkugel und schräge Schulternähte) verbinden oder von rechts im Matratzenstich zusammennähen. Dieser empfiehlt sich besonders bei geraden Nähten, Bündchen und feinteiligen Farbmustern. Für die Befestigung von Blenden und Taschenbeuteln auf der Innenseite eines Strickstücks ist vielfach der Maschenstich die unauffälligste Lösung.

Für die Ärmel gibt es verschiedene Methoden des Einsetzens.

Beim Ärmel ohne Armkugel wird der Ärmel mit der Mitte der oberen Ärmelkante auf die Schulternaht geheftet und in der angegebenen Armausschnitthöhe am Vorder- und Rückteil eingenäht, danach werden die Ärmel- und Seitennähte geschlossen.

Beim Ärmel mit L-Ausschnitt wird die Mitte der oberen Ärmelkante auf die Schulternaht geheftet und der Ärmel bis zum Beginn der Abnahmen für die Armausschnitte in die Armausschnittkante eingenäht. Anschließend werden die letzten geraden Reihen des Ärmels mit den Abnahmen der Armausschnittkante verbunden.

Beim Ärmel mit Armkugel werden zuerst die Seitennähte von Vorder- und Rückenteil geschlossen. Die Mitte der Armkugel wird auf die Schulternaht geheftet, danach wird der Ärmel mit eingehaltener Weite in den Armausschnitt genäht.

Die Seiten- und Unterarmnähte schließen. Die Taschenblenden und Taschenbeutel festnähen. Die Knöpfe in Höhe der Knopflöcher festnähen. Gerippte Bündchen oder Halsblenden sowie kraus rechts gestrickte Abschnitte dürfen nicht gedämpft werden.

Abkürzungen

Abk	abketten
abn	abnehmen
Anf	Anfang
anschl	anschlagen
arb	arbeiten
bds	beidseitig
Fbe	Farbe
Hinr	Hinreihe
li	links
M	Masche
mark	markieren
Ndl	Nadel
Nr.	Nummer
R	Reihe
Rde	Runde
re	rechts
Rückr	Rückreihe
seitl	seitlich
str	stricken
U	Umschlag
verschr	verschränkt
vord	vordere
wdhl	wiederholen
ZN	Zopfnadel
zun	zunehmen
zus-str	zusammenstricken

Abkürzungen in den Häkelanleitungen

Wlm	Eine Lm die nach dem Wenden der Arbeit oder am Anf einer R gehäkelt wird, diese Lm zählt nicht als M;
Lm	Luftmasche
Fm	Feste Masche
Km	Kettmasche
St	einfaches Stäbchen
DST	ein doppeltes Stäbchen.
Lm-Zw	Luftmaschenzwischenraum

Alle im Magazin angegebenen Knöpfe und Bänder sind erhältlich bei
Groves & Banks
Eastern Bypass
Thame
Oxfordshire
OX9 3FU
www.grovesltd.co.uk
groves@stockistenquiries.co.uk

Bedecked Haberdashery
The Coach House
Barningham Park
RICHMOND
DL11 7DW
Tel: +44 (0)1833 621 451
eMail:Judith.lewis@bedecked.co.uk
www.bedecked.co.uk

SCHWIERIGKEITSGRADE
Orientierungshilfe

⭐ **Für Anfänger geeignet**
Diese gerade gestrickten Modelle sind für Anfänger geeignet, die die Grundkenntnisse beherrschen.

⭐⭐ **Stricktechnisch einfach**
Einfache, gerade gestrickte Modelle mit leichten und unterschiedlichen Techniken der Formgebung.

⭐⭐⭐ **Für erfahrene Stricker geeignet**
Diese Modelle verwenden anspruchsvollere Schnitte mit farbigen oder gemusterten Techniken.

⭐⭐⭐⭐ **Für Fortgeschrittene**
Stricktechnisch aufwändig, mit schwierigeren Maschen und Schnitten und herausfordernden Techniken.

GRÖSSE DER MODELS
Tiegan trägt für 5-6 Jahre
Janae trägt für 9-10 Jahre

Hinweise zur Pflege

Sie haben sicher bemerkt, dass sich in der letzten Saison die Symbole zur Pflege auf den Banderolen und Farbkarten geändert haben. Wir haben die Symbole aktualisiert, sie sollen Ihnen eine Hilfe sein zur weiteren Pflege für Ihre gestrickten oder gehäkelten Modelle. Unten sehen Sie die Symbole mit einer kurzen Erklärung.

Symbole für die Waschmaschine

Symbole für die Handwäsche

Symbole für chemisches Reinigen

Symbole zum Bügeln

Symbol für das Verwenden von Bleichmitteln

Symbole für den Trockner

Grössentabelle

Wenn Sie ein Kinderdesign stricken, möchten wir, dass Sie mit dem Aussehen und der Haptik des fertigen Kleidungsstücks zufrieden sind. Dies alles beginnt mit der Größe und Passform des von Ihnen gewählten Designs. Um Ihnen zu helfen, die richtige Passform für Ihr Kind zu erreichen, sehen Sie sich bitte die Größentabelle unten an.

Bei den Maßen in der Tabelle handelt es sich um Körpermaße, nicht um Konfektionsgrößen. Bitte beachten Sie daher die Maße, die Ihnen dabei helfen, die richtige Größe zu finden.

STANDARD GRÖSSEN FÜR KINDER

ALTER	3 - 4 Jahre	5 - 6 Jahre	7 - 8 Jahre	9 - 10 Jahre	11 - 12 Jahre	
Körperlänge	98 - 104	110 - 116	122 - 128	134 - 140	146 - 152	cm
Für Brustumfang	31	34	36	39	42	cm
Für Taillenumfang	30	32	34	36	38	cm

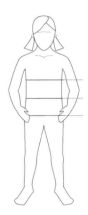

GRÖSSEN UND HINWEISE ZUM DIAGRAMM

Die Anleitungen wurden für die kleinste Größe geschrieben. Wo sie variieren, stehen die nächsten Größen in Klammern hinter der kleinsten Größe. Steht nur eine Zahl da, gilt sie für alle Größen. Bei den meisten Anleitungen ist am Ende ein "Schnittdiagramm" des fertigen Kleidungsstücks und seiner Maße gezeichnet - siehe Abbildung rechts. Das Maß am unteren Rand jedes "Schnittdiagramms" zeigt die Breite des Kleidungsstücks 2,5 cm unterhalb des Armausschnittes. Um Ihnen bei der Auswahl der Größe des zu strickenden Strickstücks zu helfen, lesen Sie bitte die Anleitung zur Größenbestimmung. Im Allgemeinen ist bei den meisten Designs die seitliche Länge des Kleidungsstücks genauso breit wie im Brustbereich. Einige Designs haben jedoch die Form einer "A-Linie" oder einen ausgestellten Rand, und in diesen Fällen ist die untere Kante breiter als die Brustbreite.

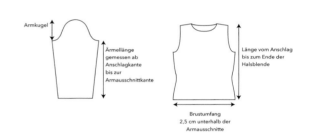

DIE RICHTIGE GRÖSSE FINDEN

Für maximalen Komfort und um die richtige Passform bei der Wahl der zu strickenden Größe zu gewährleisten, befolgen Sie bitte die folgenden Tipps, wenn Sie die Größe Ihres Babys oder Kindes überprüfen. Messen Sie so nah wie möglich am Körper über der Unterwäsche, aber ziehen Sie das Maßband nicht zu fest!

Länge
Wird vom Scheitel bis zu den Füßen des Kindes gemessen, wenn es gerade liegt oder steht.

Brustumfang
Wird unterhalb der Arme um den ganzen Brustkorb gemessen.

Taillenumfang
Wird um die natürliche Taillenlinie knapp oberhalb des Hüftknochens gemessen.

Hüftumfang
Wird um die breiteste Stelle des Gesäß gemessen.

Wenn Sie Ihr Kind nicht messen möchten, messen Sie die Größen des Lieblingspullovers vom Kind aus, dessen Passform richtig ist.

Unsere Größen sind vergleichbar mit den Konfektionsgrößen der Einzelhändler in den Einkaufsstraßen. Wenn der Lieblingspullover für 6 Monate oder 3 Jahre ist, dann sollten unsere Angaben für 6 Monate- oder 3 Jahre ungefähr übereinstimmen. Messen Sie den Lieblingspullover aus und vergleichen Sie die Maße mit den Angaben im Größendiagramm am Ende der Anleitung.
Wenn die richtige Größe gefunden wurde, stellen Sie sicher, dass die Maschenprobe stimmt.
Ist sie zu locker ist, wird das Strickstück größer sein als beim Schnitt angegeben, und die Garnmenge reicht nicht aus, ist sie zu fest, wird das Strickstück zu klein, und es ist noch Wolle übrig. Das Nichteinhalten der richtigen Maschenprobe verändert auch die Griffigkeit des Strickstücks.
Da Sie Geld und Zeit in das Stricken investiert haben, ist es wirklich sinnvoll, die Maschenprobe anzufertigen, bevor Sie mit Ihrem Projekt beginnen.

Share your sense of style with cute and cosy matching Mode fashion...

Mode Collection One,
011 Tunic

Snowdrop

Big Wool Textures,
Dream

Dream

Soft Boucle & Merino Aria,
Scarf

Fifi

Mode Collection One,
017 Beanie & 018 Scarf

Flo | Tallulah

Soft Boucle & Merino Aria,
Teddy Coat

Teddy

Mode Collection Two,
009 Cable Bobble Sweater

Luna

Mode Collection Three,
013 Cardigan

Silver

Mode Collection Three,
001 Poncho

Moon

Mode 4 Projects
Alpaca Classic,
Blue Haze

Alaska

Soft Boucle & Merino Aria,
Teddy Gilet

Bear

Mode Collection Two,
006 Striped Tank

Ivy

Big Wool Textures,
Haze

Haze

Mode 4 Projects
Brushed Fleece, **Polar**

Cub

Mode Collection Three,
008 Beanie

Rosie

DISTRIBUTORS

AUSTRALIA: Morris and Sons
Level 1, 234 Collins Street, Melbourne Vic 3000
Tel: 03 9654 0888　**Web:** morrisandsons.com.au

AUSTRALIA: Morris and Sons
50 York Street, Sydney NSW 2000
Tel: 02 92998588　**Web:** morrisandsons.com.au

AUSTRIA: DMC
5 Avenue de Suisse BP 189, Illzach (France)
Email: info-FR@dmc.com

BELGIUM: DMC
5 Avenue de Suisse BP 189, Illzach (France)
Email: info-FR@dmc.com

CANADA: Sirdar USA Inc.
406 20th Street SE, Hickory, North Carolina, USA 28602
Tel: 828 404 3705　**Email:** sirdarusa@sirdar.co.uk

CHINA: Commercial Agent Mr Victor Li,
Email: victor.li@mezcrafts.com

CHINA: Shanghai Yujun CO.LTD.
Room 701 Wangjiao Plaza, No.175 Yan'an Road, 200002 Shanghai, China
Tel: +86 2163739785　**Email:** jessechang@vip.163.com

DENMARK: Carl J. Permin A/S
Egegaardsvej 28 DK-2610 Rødovre
Tel: (45) 36 36 89 89　**Email:** permin@permin.dk
Web: www.permin.dk

ESTONIA: Mez Crafts Estonia OÜ
Helgi tee 2, Peetri alevik, Tallinn, 75312 Harjumaa
Tel: +372 6 306 759　Email: info.ee@mezcrafts.com
Web: www.mezcrafts.ee

FINLAND: Prym Consumer Finland Oy
Huhtimontie 6, 04200 KERAVA
Tel: +358 9 274871 **Email:** sales.fi@prym.com

FRANCE: DMC
5 Avenue de Suisse BP 189, Illzach (France)
Email: info-FR@dmc.com

GERMANY: DMC
5 Avenue de Suisse BP 189, Illzach (France)
Email: info-DE@dmc.com

HOLLAND: G. Brouwer & Zn B.V.
Oudhuijzerweg 69, 3648 AB Wilnis
Tel: 0031 (0) 297-281 557　**Email:** info@gbrouwer.nl

ICELAND: Carl J. Permin A/S
Egegaardsvej 28, DK-2610 Rødovre
Tel: (45) 36 72 12 00　**Email:** permin@permin.dk
Web: www.permin.dk

ITALY: DMC
Via Magenta 77/5, Rho (Milano)
Email: info-IT@dmc.com

JAPAN: DMC KK
Santo Building 7F, 13, Kanda Konya Cho, Chiyodaku, 101-0035 , Tokyo
Email: ouchi@dmc-kk.com

KOREA: My Knit Studio
3F, 59 Insadong-gil, Jongno-gu, 03145, Seoul
Tel: 82-2-722-0006　**Email:** myknit@myknit.com
Web: www.myknit.com

LATVIA: Latvian Crafts
12-2, Jurģu street, LV-2011
Tel: +371 37 126326825　**Email:** vjelkins@latviancrafts.lv
Web: www.latviancrafts.lv

LEBANON: y.knot
Saifi Village, Mkhalissiya Street 162, Beirut
Tel: (961) 1 992211　**Email:** y.knot@cyberia.net.lb

LUXEMBOURG: DMC
5 Avenue de Suisse BP 189, Illzach (France)
Email: info-FR@dmc.com

NEW ZEALAND: Trendy Trims
7 Angle Street, Onehunga, Auckland, New Zealand
Email: trendy@trendytrims.co.nz **Web:** trendytrims.co.nz

NORWAY: Carl J. Permin A/S
Andersrudveien 1, 1914, Ytre Enebakk
Tel: 23 16 35 30　**Email:** permin@permin.dk
Web: www.permin.dk

PORTUGAL: DMC
P. Ferrocarriles Catalanes, 117 oficina 34, Cornellá de llobregat, 08940
Email: info-PT @dmc.com

RUSSIA: Family Hobby
Zelenograd, Haus 1505, Raum III, 124683
Email: tv@fhobby.ru　**Web:** www.family-hobby.ru

SOUTH AFRICA: Arthur Bales LTD
62 4th Avenue, Linden 2195
Tel: (27) 11 888 2401　**Email:** info@arthurbales.co.za
Web: www.arthurbales.co.za

SPAIN: DMC
P. Ferrocarriles Catalanes, 117 oficina 34, Cornellá de llobregat, 08940
Email: info-SP @dmc.com

SWEDEN: Carl J. Permin A/S
Skaraborgsvägen 35C, 3tr, Borås
Tel: 33 12 77 10　**Email:** sverige@permin.dk
Web: www.permin.dk

SWITZERLAND: DMC
5 Avenue de Suisse BP 189, Illzach (France)
Email: info-DE@dmc.com

U.S.A.: Sirdar USA Inc
406 20th Street SE, Hickory, North Carolina, USA 28602
Tel: 828 404 3705　**Email:** sirdarusa@sirdar.co.uk
Web: www.sirdar.com

U.K: Rowan
Flanshaw Lane, Alverthorpe, Wakefield, WF2 9ND, United Kingdom
Tel: 01924 371501　**Email:** mail@knitrowan.com

For more stockists in all countries please logon to **www.knitrowan.com**